INSPIRED BY THE
COUNTRY
FOOD • CRAFTS • DECORATING

INSPIRED BY THE
COUNTRY
FOOD • CRAFTS • DECORATING

A treasury of creative ideas, with 130 step-by-step projects for interiors, natural
decorations, crafts and mouthwatering food, all shown in over 750 photographs

liz trigg • tessa evelegh • stewart & sally walton

southwater

This edition is published by Southwater, an imprint of Anness Publishing Ltd,
Blaby Road, Wigston, Leicestershire LE18 4SE

Email: info@anness.com

Web: www.southwaterbooks.com; www.annesspublishing.com

If you like the images in this book and would like to investigate using them for publishing, promotions
or advertising, please visit our website www.practicalpictures.com for more information.

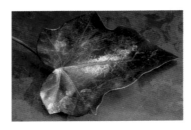

Publisher: Joanna Lorenz
Project Editor: Lindsay Porter
Designer: Janet James
Photographer for *Country Decorating*: James Duncan
Photographs on pp 6–9, 14, 15, 36, 37, 56 and 57 by Steve Tanner
Stylist for *Country Decorating*: Tessa Evelegh
Photographer and Stylist for *Country Crafts and Flowers* and *Country Cooking*: Michelle Garrett
Illustrator: Nadine Wickenden
Production Controller: Christine Ni

ETHICAL TRADING POLICY

At Anness Publishing we believe that business should be conducted in an ethical and ecologically sustainable way,
with respect for the environment and a proper regard to the replacement of the natural resources we employ.
As a publisher, we use a lot of wood pulp in high-quality paper for printing, and that wood commonly comes from
spruce trees. We are therefore currently growing more than 750,000 trees in three Scottish forest plantations:
Berrymoss (130 hectares/320 acres), West Touxhill (125 hectares/305 acres) and Deveron Forest (75 hectares/
185 acres). The forests we manage contain more than 3.5 times the number of trees employed each year in
making paper for the books we manufacture.
Because of this ongoing ecological investment programme, you, as our customer, can have the pleasure and
reassurance of knowing that a tree is being cultivated on your behalf to naturally replace the materials used to make
the book you are holding.
Our forestry programme is run in accordance with the UK Woodland Assurance Scheme (UKWAS) and will be
certified by the internationally recognized Forest Stewardship Council (FSC). The FSC is a non-government
organization dedicated to promoting responsible management of the world's forests. Certification ensures forests are
managed in an environmentally sustainable and socially responsible way. For further information about this scheme,
go to www.annesspublishing.com/trees

Previously published as *Country Inspirations*

PUBLISHER'S NOTE

Although the advice and information in this book are believed to be accurate and true at the time of going to press,
neither the authors nor the publisher can accept any legal responsibility or liability for any errors or omissions
that may have been made nor for any inaccuracies nor for any loss, harm or injury that comes about from
following instructions or advice in this book.

Contents

Country Style

Picture a house in the countryside on a bright autumn day, smoke wafting from the chimney into a brilliant blue sky. There are trees that have turned glorious shades of yellow and orange and there is a chill in the wind. Cats are asleep in shafts of sunlight, ignoring the birds that chatter on the rooftop. On a summer day, the arch over the gate will be covered with roses, and hollyhocks will stretch up the white walls past the open windows from which muslin billows out, caught by the warm breeze. ❧ Step inside the house and smell bread baking in the range; leave your boots on the rack and walk across the cool flagstones. Sink into a comfortable chair by the scrubbed pine table and look around at stencilled patterns, crocheted lace, gleaming copper pans and wooden spoons. This is the country that we see in our dreams, and if our waking hours are passed in a high-speed, high-pressure city environment, these dreams have an added seductive quality. Rosy images of the pastoral are potent symbols of a way of life that seems somehow gentler, less stressful and more natural than the urban routine. As the pressures of late twentieth-century living mount, we want to put some of that country tranquility back into our lives. One of the easiest ways of doing this is to recreate some elements of country style in the home, providing a restful and welcoming environment to come back to. You don't have to live in a cottage to create the cottage look: the look comes as much from a way of thinking as from a way of living. ❧ This book shows you how to get into that way of thinking, and how to channel it into creative projects that will bring something of the dream of country living into your home — whether that is a farmhouse or a flat. But it's not just the end-product of your creativity that you will value; in the process of designing and making country-style artefacts and effects you will find a satisfaction and sense of peace that are the real goals of country style.

BELOW: *beautiful practical of patchw typical of country st*

Achieving a Country Look

Country style has many interpretations and all over the world there are towns-people who dream of a calmer way of life in a place where traffic doesn't bustle, food has more flavour and night skies are filled with stars, not neon. This may be an idealized picture, but it has an underlying truth: country life is still governed by seasonal changes, not man-made deadlines. ❧ Country homes are alive, growing and comfortable and country decorating is for living in, not just looking at. Many of the effects that we think of as talismans of country style have an eminently practical function. ❧ Country style may vary a

lot, according to nationality and the local climate, but there is a core of recognizable elements. It is a home-made, functional, comfortable style. There is often a big kitchen area, with a large scrubbed pine table and an assortment of comfortable chairs. Country kitchens can be a riot of pattern and colour, where the dresser is stacked with displays of china and the beams are hung with baskets-full of drying flowers and herbs. Gleaming copper pots and pans should never be

ABOVE: *Although several motifs are present in this room, the restricted use of colour pulls the whole look together.*

hidden away in cupboards, so use butcher's hooks to display them out of 'head banging' reach. Floors need to be practical, tough and easy to keep clean, so floorboards, flagstones, linoleum or cork tiles are the favourite choices, and they can all be softened with washable cotton dhurries or rag rugs. ❧ The food prepared in the country kitchen is hearty and nourishing, and is prepared from the produce of the season – warming roasts and stews in the winter and light, fresh vegetable flans or fruit tarts in the summer. Locally grown produce – organic, if not from your own garden – will taste immeasurably

better if it is a seasonal treat rather than a year-round staple. ❧ Through-out the home, flower arrangements take their cue from nature and are combined with other organic materials to provide a more casual, spontaneous look than hot-house blooms. A ginger jar that has been in the family for years stands alongside an enamel jug filled with flowers from yesterday's walk. You might choose to float flowerheads on a glass plate, or collect supple twigs to form a heart-shaped wreath wrapped with trailing ivy. The colours of autumn may be represented by gourds, vegetables and dried seedheads. ❧ The country house is not a fashion statement, and its colour schemes should reflect the natural colour in the landscape; these need not be dull, bland and safe; they can be as rich as autumn, with touches of brilliance, or warm as a summer pasture filled with buttercups or a field of ripe corn. ❧ The house responds to personal touches; a painted border may still be there in 50 years, so paint it thoughtfully. Make time in your life to be creative, whether it be with stencilling, floor-painting or embroidery. All home-made crafts add richness to the home and give you a sense of personal achievement that money cannot buy. ❧ There are step-by-step projects here to suit all levels of experience and creative ability. You may feel daunted by embroidery but more confident about making patterns in tin with a hammer and nail; unsure about flower arranging, but able to pop a few dried flowerheads into a terracotta pot.

BELOW: Decorative panels can transform a piece of furniture. If you are not confident about painting free-hand, stencilling is a simpler option.

Whatever you choose, rest assured that all the projects have been designed to give maximum effect for minimum effort. If you want to ring the changes very quickly on your walls, use a colour glaze with a foam-block print or stencilled border. Giving floorboards the limed look requires the hard work of sanding first, but the painting can be done and

Patchwork
soften a
hair,
ide a
use for
s and
of fabric.

dried in an afternoon. If you have considered laying cork tiles, then stain half of them black and make a real impact with a chequer-board floor. ❧ When it comes to choosing materials, or pieces of furniture to decorate, take a tip from the squirrel and start hoarding! There are so many second-hand stores, car boot sales and jumble sales around, and if you buy things that have potential, you will always have something to hand when the creative mood strikes. It can be amazingly difficult to find a wooden tray or a nice tin can when you want one, so have a 'potential' corner in the loft or the shed, and keep it well stocked! ❧ On a very practical note, there has been a major change in materials for home-decorating recently, with the arrival of water-based paint products. There is no longer any need for solvents to clean brushes; they rinse out under the tap. The biggest bonus of this revolution is that decorating time has been cut in half. Water-based products dry very quickly, and this is especially useful when applying many coats of varnish to painted furniture. The rule to remember is not to mix oil and water, so if you tint varnish for an antique effect, mix acrylics with water-based clear varnish or oil colour with traditional varnish. ❧ Whether you go for the total country look for your home, or just a few details, always try to decorate in a way that is sympathetic to the character and age of your house. Use the best features, like an interestingly shaped window, as focal points; be courageous about removing a ghastly fireplace, or disguising oppressively heavy beams. Your home should please you, and country style is about personal touches, natural materials, warmth and comfort. So, follow your instincts and enjoy the charm of country life.

COUNTRY
Decorating

STEWART AND SALLY WALTON

Walls and Floors

*A coat of paint or an interesting floor covering will
transform any room, and will set the scene
for the total country look. Transform your walls
with stencils or a hand-painted frieze;
foam-block stamps look as authentic as hand-blocked
wall paper, and are a fraction of the cost.
For floors, try limed-look floorboards, cork tiling,
or a trompe-l'oeil dhurrie.*

The Country Palette

Colour has a great influence on us: it can affect our moods quite dramatically. Choose your palette from nature's harmonies, avoiding artificially brilliant colours. It would be a mistake to think that natural colours are all shades of beige; just think of autumn and the huge variety of yellows, oranges and scarlets that mingle among the trees.

When painting the walls country-style it is best to avoid a perfect, even finish – go instead for a patchy, glowing, colour-washed effect. By doing this you can use strong colour, but in a transparent way that is not as heavy as solid colour. Don't avoid strong colours like brick red, deep green or dusky blue. The furniture, rugs, pictures, ornaments, cushions and curtains will all combine to absorb the strength of the wall colour and dilute its power. If your rooms are dark, use the strong colours below dado-rail height only, with a creamy, light colour on the upper walls and ceiling. Darker colours can be very cosy in a large room, but if you want a room to look bigger it would be best to stick to a lighter scheme, and use a stencil or free-hand border to add colour and interest.

If mixing your own paint is too daunting a prospect, you could go for one of the new 'historic' ranges made by specialist producers. These paints are a lot more expensive than ordinary brands, but the colour ranges are designed to harmonize with antiques, natural building materials and old textiles, and if your budget can stretch to them, they really are wonderful.

If your courage fails and you choose white walls, think about highlighting the woodwork. Paint a deep, rich colour on the skirtings and the window-and door-frames, allow it to dry and then

ABOVE: *Colours derived from nature are not necessarily sombre. Think of clear blue skies or a field of wildflowers.*

paint a light colour on top. Use a damp cloth to wipe off some of the topcoat, and sandpaper to lift colour that has dried. This will give you an effect of flashes of brilliance to add warmth to the room.

Choose natural colours that make you happy, and remember that country-style decorating is not about having everything matching. You don't need co-ordinating curtains, carpets and lampshades. On the contrary, the more eclectic the choice, the more stunning the effect can often be.

Giving your home the country look requires attention to the basics – the walls and floors. Get these right and the rest is easy. A bare room with powdery wall-paint, stencilling and a stripped, limed floor has a real country feeling, whereas no amount of folk artefacts and rustic furniture can transform to 'country' a tastefully wallpapered, corniced and thick-pile carpeted drawing room!

The ideal way to begin would be to clear the house, remove all the old wallpaper

and carpets and start from scratch this is a luxury that few can afford more practical to think in terms of room at a time, repainting the wa adding one of the country-style fl that are featured in this chapter.

This chapter shows how the basic elements of a room can be change make it feel more individual. Wh paint, stencil or print on your wal truly become your own, and this happens with wallpaper, however you are at hanging it! We someti suggest cheating a little: roughen smooth surfaces, wiping off more than is put on, or stencilling unev for a worn-away look. You can't w hundred years for this to occur na

The ideas for the projects have be inspired by folk art and by real-li examples of country decorating of homes. There has been a recent rev interest in the subject and it is no possible to buy kits to age practic anything, with a plethora of equip required for the job.

Whatever you choose for your wall floor, it is important to see them i terms of a backdrop for your own and possessions. Paintings, mirror lamps, plants, shelves, rugs and furniture will all add to the final A painted border may appear to b dominant in an empty room, but effect will be much more subtle w the furnishings, accessories and pe details have been added.

Remember that country style is m about relaxation, comfort and harr than precision and fashion; this is type of decorating that is a pleasu involve yourself in, so enjoy the p as well as the result.

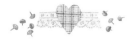

CLOCKWISE FROM TOP LEFT: *The walls and floors have been coated with tinted varnish to simulate the patina of age. Deep, brick red is bold, yet warm in a sitting room. The soft colours of this crazy patchwork quilt are punctuated with vibrant stitching.*

Brushed-out Colour Glaze

This soft, patchy wall finish is pure country. It's traditionally achieved using either a very runny colour-wash, or an oil-based glaze tinted with oil colour, over eggshell paint. This project gives the same effect, but is easier to achieve.

The unusual element in the glaze is wallpaper paste, which is mixed in the usual way before the addition of PVA glue. The wallpaper paste adds a translucency to the colour and the PVA seals the surface when dry. To tint the glaze you can use powder, gouache or acrylic paint, mixed with a small amount of water first, so that it blends easily.

Use a large decorator's brush to apply the glaze, dabbing glaze on to the wall about five times within an arm's reach. Then use light, random strokes to sweep the glaze across the area, to use up the dabs and cover the area. Move along the wall, blending each area with the next.

This is a very cheap way of painting a room, so you can afford to mix up more glaze than you will use, and throw some away. This is preferable to running out before you finish, because it is so difficult to match the original colour. A litre / 1¾ pints of glaze will cover almost 40 square metres/yards.

MATERIALS

*PVA glue
wallpaper paste
acrylic, gouache or powder paint,
to colour the glaze
large decorator's brush*

1

Prepare your wall-surface: ideally it should be an off-white vinyl silk, but any plain, light colour will do, if it is clean. Wash old paint with sugar soap and leave it to dry. Mix up the glaze, using 1 part PVA glue, 5 parts water and ¼ part wallpaper paste. Tint it with three 20 cm / 8 in squirts from an acrylic or gouache tube, or about 15 ml / 1 tbsp of powder paint. Vary the intensity of colour to your own taste. Experiment on scrap lining paper painted with the same background colour as your walls. Get the feel of the glaze and brush, and adjust the colour at this stage if necessary.

2

Begin applying the glaze in an area of the room that will be hidden by furniture or pictures; as your technique improves you will be painting the more obvious areas. Start near the top of the wall, dabbing glaze on with the brush and then sweeping it over the surface with random strokes, as described previously.

3

The effect is streaky and the brushstro show, but they can be softened before are completely dry. After about 5 mi brush the surface lightly with your bru don't use any glaze. The brush will pi any surplus glaze on the surface and l softer, less streaky effect. When wor on edges and corners, apply the glaze then brush it away from the corner or You will still find that the colour ma more concentrated in some places, b will all look very different when the is furnished.

'Powdery' Paint Finish for Walls

You may need to 'rough-up' your walls a bit to achieve this look; this is easily done with a tub of filler, a spatula and some rough-grade sandpaper. Think of it as a reversal of the usual preparations!

int finish imitates the opaque, our and powdery bloom of er, the wall finish most used he invention of emulsion The joy of decorating with this ry finish' paint, is that it can be rectly on concrete, plaster or board – indeed almost any surface out lining paper or special oats. The paint is diluted with o the consistency required, and is on with a large brush. Mistakes is can be wiped off with a damp nd the paint is a pleasure to use. about two hours to dry, and the lightens considerably as it does so, ne final effect is revealed – a soft ry surface of matt colour that will nstant warmth to any room.

stressed' plaster effect has a ngly country feel. Perhaps we e that real country folk didn't he time or inclination to decorate rfect finish; for whatever reasons, something very comfortable walls with irregular surfaces and aint.

MATERIALS

*Polyfilla or similar filler
spatula
rough-grade sandpaper
rats 'Mediterranean Palette'
paint in shade 'Asia'
large decorator's brush*

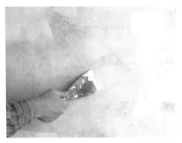

1

Prepare the walls by stripping off any wallpaper down to the bare plaster. Spread the filler irregularly with the spatula to simulate the uneven texture of old plaster. Use thin layers, applied randomly from different directions. Don't worry about overdoing the effect; you can always rub it back with sandpaper when it's dry, after about an hour.

2

Blend the dried filler into the original wall surface using the sandpaper, leaving rougher areas for a more obvious distressed effect. Mix the paint with water in the ratio 2 parts water to 1 part paint.

3

Begin painting at ceiling height. The paint is likely to splash a bit, so protect any surfaces with an old sheet or decorator's cloth. Use the paintbrush in a random way, rather than in straight lines, and expect a patchy effect – it will fade as the paint dries. The second coat needs to be stronger, so use less water in the mixture. Stir the paint well; it should have the consistency of single cream.

Apply the second coat in the same way, working the brush into any cracks or rough plaster areas. Two hours later the 'bloom' of the powdery finish will have appeared. The element of surprise makes decorating with this paint exciting, especially as the final texture is so mellow and effective at covering, but not concealing, the irregularities of the wall's surface. We used this surface as a base for the stencilled border on the following page:

Stencilled Border

Stencilling tends to spread around the house like a climbing plant, appearing round doorways and winding along picture rails, up staircases and across floors! It is a delightful and habit-forming activity and it's extremely difficult to be a minimalist when it comes to stencilling.

The design used for this border came from a Rhode Island house that was built and decorated in the eighteenth century. Stencilling was an extremely popular means of decorating interiors, and stencils were used to create pillars and friezes as well as all-over patterns, with as many as seven different designs on a single wall.

A border design like this one is perfectly suited for use above a dado-rail, but there is no reason why you should not use it at picture-rail, or skirting-board height, or even as a frame around a window. Or you may not have a dado-rail but still like the

effect of a wall divided in this way. In this case it is a simple matter of marking the division with paint or varnish.

Use a plumb-line and a long ruler to divide the wall, marking the line in pencil. The wall below the line can be painted a darker shade, or, if you are using the 'Mediterranean Palette' colour, a coat of clear satin varnish will darken the colour and add a sheen. The stencilled border will visually integrate the two sections of wall and soften the edges between them. If you vary the depth of stencilled colour, it will look naturally faded by time.

MATERIALS

tracing paper
Mylar or stencil card
spray adhesive
scalpel or craft knife
masking tape
Brats Mediterranean Palette p
in shade 'Asia' (optional)
varnish in shade 'Antique Pi
household painthrush
stencil paint
stencil brush

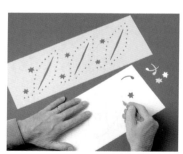

1

Trace and enlarge the pattern from the template section. Stick it on the Mylar using spray adhesive. Use a scalpel or craft knife to cut out the stencil carefully. Repair any mistakes with masking tape and always use a very sharp blade which will give you the most control when cutting. Peel off the remaining tracing paper.

2

If desired, prepare the powdery paint on the previous page, then paint the w wall in 'Asia'. Paint the lower half of th with a coat of Antique Pine tinted va Use random brush strokes for a rough

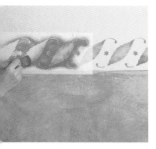

3
---

a light spray of adhesive to the back of
…ncil and leave it to dry for 5 minutes.
…n the stencil at a corner and paint the
…colour. Use the paint very sparingly,
…g the brush on absorbent kitchen paper
…e using it on the wall. You can always
…er a light area to darken it later, but
…s paint on the brush will cause blobs,
…ced through to the back of the stencil.
…the stencil and wipe any excess paint
…he pattern edges before positioning it
…gside the stencilling. Continue along
…p of the dado-rail until the first colour
is complete.

4

…ncil paint is fast-drying, so you can
…ediately begin to add the next colour,
…g at the same point as you did with the
…. Work your way around the border,
…membering to wipe the stencil clean
as you go.

Free-hand Frieze with Half-gloss to Dado Height

This project combines the idea of dividing up the wall with textures and colours, and the free-hand painting of a vine frieze. The frieze will take some planning and preparation to achieve the casual free-hand effect, but the finished painting will look effortless and be unique.

A coat of gloss paint below the dado-rail will provide a practical, tough, wipe-clean surface where you most need it, and the gloss gives the colour a marvellous reflective shine. The lighter colour above the dado has a matt texture and the shade is reminiscent of cream straight from the dairy. If you don't have a dado-rail dividing your wall, this project is just as effective on a plain wall.

The secret of painting free-hand curves on a vertical surface, is to steady your hand on a mahlstick, which is quite simply a piece of dowel about 45 cm / 18 in long. Make a small pad of cotton wool at one end, cover it with a small square of cotton or muslin and secure it with a rubber band. Use the stick by pressing the pad against the wall with your spare hand, holding the stick free of the wall. Rest your brush hand lightly on it to prevent wobbles and jerks. Practise the curves with the mahlstick before starting the frieze, but remember that the charm of hand-painting is its variability, so relax and enjoy yourself.

*National Trust paint in shades
51 (Sudbury Yellow)
emulsion, 14 (Berrington Blue)
full gloss and 43 (Eating Room
Red) oil eggshell
paint-roller and tray
gloss-roller
2.5 cm/1 in decorator's brush
masking tape,
if necessary
chalk line or ruler
chalk
stencil card with design*

*medium-weight card
scalpel or craft knife
1 cm/½ in square-ended artist's
brush
gonache paint in Indian red and
raw sienna
45 cm/18 in length of dowelling
(of pencil thickness)
small wad of cotton wool
square of cotton fabric
rubber band
number 6 round-ended artist's
brush*

1

…yellow emulsion to the prepared wall
…he paint-roller, from ceiling to dado.
…ue gloss colour between the dado and
…g, using the gloss-roller. Using the
…ggshell paint, and the 2.5 cm/1 in
…aint the skirting board and the dado-
…f you have one. Use masking tape,
…cessary, to give a clean line. Use a
…ne or ruler to draw light chalk guide-
…marking out the depth of the frieze.

2

Using your chosen stencil, lightly mark
out the position of the frieze by drawing
through the stencil.

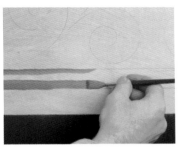

3

Paint the thick and thin lines, using the
square-ended brush, flat and on its side, and
the gouache paints. To add variety to the
line, mix up two different shades of the same
colour and use both randomly.

4

…ke up your mahlstick as described
on the previous page.

5

Paint in the curved stems, using the round-
ended brush and gouache, supporting your
hand on the mahlstick. Try to make your
movements as fluid as possible.

6

Add the bunches of grapes, above and below
the stems using the round-ended brush.
Overlap the double lines in some places:
remember that you are aiming for a hand-
painted look, not a regular-repeat pattern.

Foam-block Painting

Printing with cut-out foam blocks must be the easiest possible way to achieve the effect of hand-blocked wallpaper, and it gives an irregularity of pattern that is impossible in machine-produced papers. Another special feature of this project is the paint that we have used – a combination of wallpaper paste, PVA glue and gouache colour. This is not only cheap, but it also has a wonderful translucent quality all of its own. The combination of sponge and paint works well, because pressing and lifting the sponge emphasizes the texture that results from using a slightly sticky paint.

The best foam for cutting is high in density but still soft, such as upholsterer's foam; it needs to be at least 2.5 cm / 1 in thick. You need to be able to hold the foam firmly without distorting the printing surface.

Paint some of your background colour on to sheets of scrap paper, and then use this to try out your sponge-printing; use different densities and combinations of colour, making a note of the proportions of colour to paste in each one. This

means you will be able to mix up same colour in a larger amount wh print on the wall (although the pai go a very long way). The backgrou used here is painted using the brus out colour glaze described on page

MATERIALS

tracing paper, if necessary
upholsterer's foam off-cuts
felt-tipped pen
scalpel or craft knife
plumb-line
paper square measuring
15 × 15 cm / 6 × 6 in, or
according to your chosen spacing
wallpaper paste
PVA glue
gouache paint or ready-mixed
watercolour paint in viridian,
deep green and off-white
saucer
clear matt varnish (optional)

1

Photocopy or trace the design from the template section and cut out the shapes to leave a stencil. Trace the design on to the foam and outline it using a felt-tipped pen.

2

Cut out the shapes using a sharp sca craft knife: first cut around the patte then part the foam slightly and cut t the entire thickness.

3

Attach the plumb-line to the wall/ce join in one corner. Now turn the sq sheet of paper on the diagonal and le plumb-line fall through the centre, lir the top and bottom corners with the Make pencil dots on the wall at each Move the square down the line, mark corner points each time. Then move t along sideways. Continue until the v wall is marked with a grid of do

4

wallpaper paste and water according to manufacturer's instructions. Add PVA in the proportion 3 parts paste to 1 part A. Add a squeeze of viridian and deep reen gouache paint or ready-mixed colour, and blend the ingredients until nixed. Test the mixture on scrap paper, adding more colour if necessary.

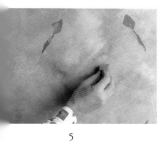

5

me paint into a saucer and dip the first ge into it. Wipe off excess paint, and print with the sponge using a light g motion. Lift and print again, using pencil dots as a positioning guide.

6

second sponge to complete the spring with leaf shapes, varying the position slightly to add life.

7

Use the dot-shaped sponge and the off-white colour to complete the motif with berries, adding the colour to the PVA mixture as before. Go over the leaves or stalks on some sprigs and let others 'float' alongside. If your walls are to be exposed to steam or splashes, or even fingerprints, you may like to protect this finish with a coat of clear matt varnish.

'Limed' Floorboards

Liming sanded wooden floorboards gives a much softer impression than stains or tinted varnishes, reminiscent of scrubbed pine kitchen-tables, washed-out wooden spoons, or driftwood bleached by the sun and the sea. If you are lucky enough to possess a sandable floor, try this easy alternative to time-consuming conventional liming. The floor can be a traditional off-white, or tinted to any pastel shade.

Raking-out the grain with a wire brush makes the channels for the paint, as well as clearing out any residual polish or varnish. If you like the wood grain to show as much as possible, wipe the surface with a damp cloth before it dries; the colour will then be concentrated in the raked-out grain of the floorboards. When the floor is dry, a coat of acrylic floor varnish will seal the colour.

MATERIALS

coarse wire brush
white emulsion paint
acrylic paint in raw umber
large decorator's brush
clean damp cloth
clear matt varnish

1

Use a wire brush to rake-out the woo
following the grain direction at all tir
Brush and vacuum the floor very caref

2

Mix up the wash, using 3 parts of water to 1 part of emulsion. Tint the colour with raw umber acrylic, or, if you prefer, use a pastel colour: pink, blue, green or yellow will all look good in the right setting, and very little of the actual colour will show. Experiment on spare boards.

3

Apply the wash with the decorator's brush, beginning in a corner at the skirting board and following the direction of the grain to the other edge.

4

Use a damp cloth to wipe away any e
paint and reveal the grain. A wet clot
just wash away the paint, so keep it
damp for this. When the floor is comp
dry, apply several coats of varnish to p
and seal the surface, allowing plent
drying time between each coat.

Hardboard Floor with Trompe-l'œil Dhurrie

It is a sad fact that not every home is blessed with handsome floorboards, to be sanded and waxed to a golden gleam. Most older houses have a mixture of new and old boards that aren't good enough to be made into a feature.

...board can be a surprisingly
...ctive solution if you're faced with a
...budget and a patchy selection of
...boards. The utilitarian appearance of
...board means it is most often used as
...elling surface below vinyl; used in
...wn right, however, and decorated
...stencils, it can look very stylish.

...ounteract the potential drabness of a
...area of hardboard this project shows
...to paint a trompe-l'oeil dhurrie in
...entre of the room, so that the plain
...d becomes the border for the
...rie. Hardboard provides a
...erfully smooth surface for painting
...he dhurrie will provide a focal point
...s guaranteed to be a talking point
...ll!

MATERIALS

newspaper
hardboard to fit the floor area
small hammer
panel pins
Stanley knife
ruler
tape measure
Crown Compatibles emulsion paint
in shades 'Dusky Blue', 'Splash
Blue' and 'Regency Cream'
2.5 cm / 1 in square-ended brush
acrylic paint in dark blue and
black
decorator's brushes
masking tape
stencil card or Mylar
scalpel or craft knife
2 cm / ½ in stencil brush
clear matt varnish

1

Lay sheets of newspaper on the floor to make
an even surface. Fit the first sheet of
hardboard into the corner nearest the door.
Hammer in panel pins 7.5 cm / 3 in apart
and 1.5 cm / ⅝ in in from the edge and
fasten the hardboard to the existing floor.

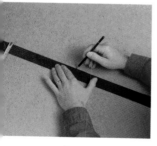

2

...e next sheet of hardboard alongside the
..., butting it hard up against the first
...:, and right up to the skirting board.
...nue laying the whole boards across the
...until you reach the point at which the
...rdboard needs to be trimmed to fit.
...re the space, at least twice, if it is not
... large or awkwardly shaped; if it is
...arly shaped, make a newsprint pattern
...e sure of getting a good fit. Cut the
...oard using a Stanley knife and a ruler
...the shiny side, then breaking along
the cut.

3

If you decide to place your dhurrie in the
centre of the room, use a tape measure to find
the centre line, and then measure out from it.
The dhurrie can be as large or small as you
like; this rug is made up of units
150 × 75 cm / 5 × 2½ feet, which you can
multiply or divide to suit your room size.
Mark the outline of the dhurrie on the floor.
Outline the area with the square-ended brush
and then fill in the Dusky Blue colour.
Leave to dry for 2 hours.

4

Tint the blue to a darker shade by adding a
squeeze of black acrylic, and then paint over
the area with a dryish brush, to give the
dhurrie a woven texture.

. . . continued

5

Trace and cut out the stencil design from the
template section. Mask off the outer patterns
with tape. Position the stencil 2 cm / ¾ in
from the edge, and stencil the central design
in Splash Blue emulsion. Remove the tape
and clean the stencil.

6

Now mask off the central pattern and
stencil the pattern on either side
in Regency Cream emulsion.

7

Position the medallion stencil along th
of the border and paint all the pattern,
for the outermost lines, in dark blue a
You can mask off these lines with tap
the previous steps.

8

Mask off the central medallion and stencil the
outer lines cream.

9

Soften the dark blue of the central medallions
with light dabs of Splash Blue emulsion.

10

Apply at least two coats of clear varn
the whole area.

Cork-tile Chequer-board Floor

Cork is a wonderful natural material that provides a warm, quiet and relatively cheap floor-covering. It has been largely confined to the kitchen and bathroom in the past, but should not be overlooked when choosing a floor for living areas.

portant to lay cork tiles on an
rface, so tack a layer of hardboard
he floorboards first. Use only
ade cork tiles. The unsealed tiles
re absorbed the coloured varnish
vo coats of clear polyurethane
with a satin finish gave a
ive seal. You may prefer a
tary brand of cork tile sealant.

MATERIALS

cork floor tiles
ood-stains in shades 'Dark
bean Oak' and 'Antique Pine'
large decorator's brush
rk-tile adhesive, if necessary
clear satin varnish

1

alf of the tiles with the Dark Jacobean
ood-stain and the remaining tiles with
ique Pine wood-stain and leave them
vernight. Measure the floor length to
sh the number of Jacobean Oak tiles
ed and cut half that number in half
ally. Begin laying tiles in the corner
ill be seen most; then, if you have to
tile at the other end, it will not be so
s. If you are using self-adhesive tiles,
simply peel off the backing.

2

Lay the contrasting tiles next, tight up against
the first row, wiping off any excess adhesive
that has been forced up between the tiles,
if you're using adhesive. Once you have laid
the two rows, measure the nearest adjoining
wall and cut half-tiles to fit the length of
that skirting as well. Stick these down.

3

Now, work to fill the floor space diagonally.
Trim the tiles at the opposite edge to fit
snugly against the skirting board. Apply two
coats of clear varnish to seal the floor. It is
important to make sure that the first coat is
bone-dry before you apply the next one, so
be patient, and let it dry overnight.

Acorn and Oak-leaf Border

A painted border can offset the austerity of plain wooden floorboards, while the pattern links different areas without dominating the room. The scale of the oak-leaf pattern can be adjusted to suit the size of your room, but try to 'think big' and enlarge the design to at least four times larger than life size, otherwise the impact will be lost.

Acorns and oak leaves have been used to decorate homes for hundreds of years, and they have a special place in country decorating. William Morris, the famous designer of the Arts and Crafts movement, used many country trees and plants in his patterns, and designed a wonderful wallpaper called 'Acorns'. Let the old saying 'Tall oaks from little acorns grow' be your inspiration, and use this painted-floor border as the basis for a warm and welcoming country-style living room.

Paint the background a dark colour and use paint with a matt finish as this will 'hold' your outline drawings better than a smooth or glossy paint. Begin at the corners and work towards the middle, using the templates as a measuring guide to work out your spacing. Once you have planned the placing of your design, work on a 60 cm/24 in area at a time, using your whole arm to make the curves, not just the wrist. This way your painting will flow in a more natural way.

MATERIALS

*medium-weight card
spray adhesive
scalpel or craft knife
masking tape
ruler
set square
National Trust paint in shade
'Off Black'
decorator's brush
white chinagraph pencil or chalk
white plate
gouache paint in yellow, sienna,
umber, etc.
soft artist's brush
plank or long ruler
lining brush
clear matt varnish*

1

Use a photocopier to enlarge the oak-le
acorn pattern from the template sectio
least four times life size (larger if you
big room). Stick the enlargement o
medium-weight card and cut around
shape with scalpel or craft knife, to le
cardboard template. Use masking tape
a ruler and set square to outline the
background colour. Apply the colour
the decorator's brush and leave to d

2

Beginning at the corner, draw around the oak-leaf template with the chinagraph pencil or chalk. Add stems or acorns to make the pattern fit around the corner, and then continue along the border. Use the template as a measuring guide, to make sure that the design fits comfortably.

3

Using a white plate as a palette, squee
several different tones of yellow, sie
umber, etc. Mix them as you pair
this adds variety.

4

n the oak-leaf shapes, using subtle
ations in colour for added interest.

5

e finishing touches and flourishes like
e leaf veining, stems and acorns.

6

straight edge, such as a plank, and a
brush to paint the lines that enclose
der about 2.5 cm/1 in from the edge.
apply 3–4 coats of clear varnish,
ng generous drying time (overnight
if possible) between coats.

Painted Canvas Floorcloth

Canvas floorcloths were first used by the early American settlers, who had travelled across the sea from Europe. They recycled canvas sailcloth, painting it to imitate the oriental carpets that were popular with the rich merchants and aristocrats in their native lands. Many layers of linseed oil were applied to the painted canvas to make them waterproof and hard-wearing.

The floorcloths were superseded by linoleum, and, unfortunately, few good old examples remain; they had no intrinsic value and were discarded when worn. Recently, however, they have undergone something of a revival. With the tough modern varnishes now available, they provide an unusual and hard-wearing alternative to the ubiquitous oriental rug.

The design for this floorcloth is based on a nineteenth-century quilt pattern called 'Sun, Moon and Stars'. The original quilt was made in very bright primary colours, but more muted shades work well for the floorcloth.

MATERIALS

craft knife or pair of sharp scissors
heavy artist's canvas (to order from art supply shops)
pencil
ruler
strong fabric adhesive
drawing pin and 1 m / 1 yd length of string
cardboard
acrylic paints in red, blue and green
medium-size square-ended artist's brush
medium-sized pointed artist's brush
varnish in shade 'Antique Pine'
household paintbrush
medium-grade sandpaper

1

Cut the canvas to the size required, a an extra 4 cm / 1 ½ in all around. D 4 cm / 1 ½ in wide border around th of the canvas and mitre the corners. fabric adhesive to the border and fol

2

Referring to the diagram in the template section, find the centre-point of the canvas and secure the string to the drawing pin at this point. You will now be able to draw the five circles needed for the design, by holding a pencil at various distances along the length of the tautly pulled string. Keep the tension on the string to draw a perfect circle.

3

Cut three differently sized cardboard triangles to make the saw-toothed edges of the two circles and the outside border. Just move the triangle along the pencil guidelines using the card as a template to draw around.

4

Cut a card circle to make a template full moons and draw them in positio trim the circle to make the crescent a the sickle moons, drawing them in p Do the same for the stars.

5

Now start filling in the red. Use the
-ended brush for larger areas and the
nted brush for outlines and fine work.

6

l in the pale blue and green circles
of colour.

7

y 3–4 coats of Antique Pine varnish
clean household brush, rubbing down
ied coat with sandpaper before applying
next one. Overnight drying is best.

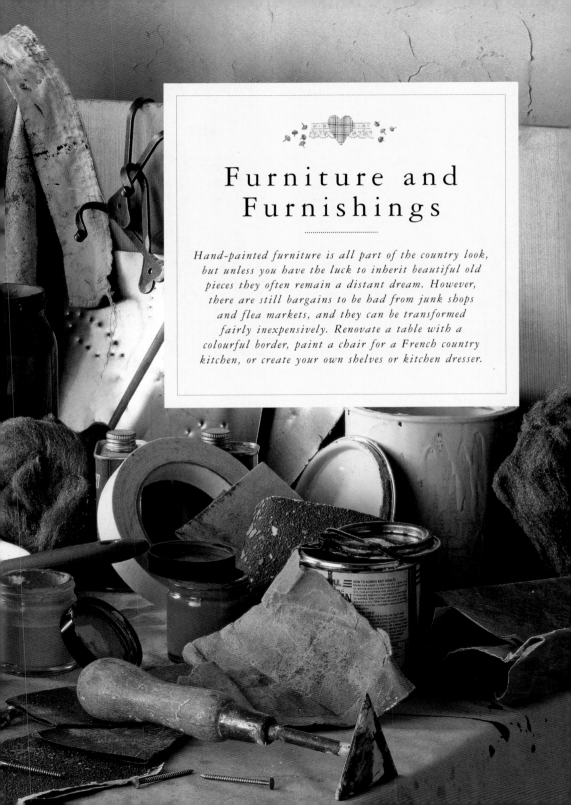

Furniture and Furnishings

Hand-painted furniture is all part of the country look, but unless you have the luck to inherit beautiful old pieces they often remain a distant dream. However, there are still bargains to be had from junk shops and flea markets, and they can be transformed fairly inexpensively. Renovate a table with a colourful border, paint a chair for a French country kitchen, or create your own shelves or kitchen dresser.

Country-style Motifs and Patterns

There are three main sources of motifs in country style – nature, local tradition and religion. Nature and the elements are the strongest influences of all and are celebrated in the decoration of rural homes throughout the world. Flowers and foliage vary according to climate; this is reflected in patterns and motifs, although some plants, like the vine for instance, have been used decoratively since classical times and are found in the art of many cultures.

Many fruit, flower and foliage motifs have symbolic meanings too, and these were incorporated into homes for their protective value in warding off evil, or for the bringing of good fortune. The rose is used as a symbol of love, both divine and earthly, and the tulip stands for prosperity. The oak leaf and acorn are associated with great potential and the future, while ivy symbolizes tenacity. The sunflower radiates warmth and is guaranteed to bring thoughts of summer to winter days.

Animals, birds and fish feature as well. Wild creatures, farm animals, faithful pets and feathered friends all find their way into country crafts and patterns. The rooster has been used since early Christian times as a symbol of faith, but it is more likely to feature in country

ABOVE: *The tulip is a popular folk motif, and symbolizes prosperity.*

decorating in celebration of his great decorative shape, coupled with his early-morning tyranny.

Cats and dogs are often commemorated in embroideries or paintings, as are horses and other farmyard friends. Patchwork quilts feature many animal and fruit designs that have been stylized to great effect, and this, in turn, has created a style of stencilling whose origins are the quilt-maker's patterns rather than the original inspiration.

Religious influences are especially noticeable in Roman Catholic countries, where there is more emphasis on the visual celebration of faith. Shrines, altars, festive decorations and votive offerings are all a part of the decoration of rural homes in countries like Mexico, Spain, Italy and France.

Harvest motifs, like the wheat she[af] the cornucopia are popular in mos[t] cultures. Fruits have been incorpor[ated] into woven and printed textiles, an[d] vegetables are a favourite subject i[n] 'theorem' paintings, a style of sten[cil] paintings used in American folk ar[t].

One of the most common country [motifs] is the heart: whether punched out [or] carved out of planks or stencilled [on] walls, the heart is everywhere. It symbolizes love and it is a uniquel[y] simple and adaptable motif. The s[hape] hardly changes at all, yet it can be [used] in many different ways without diminishing its effect. The heart h[as] been used for many centuries across [many] cultures, and yet there still seems [to be] an infinite number of new ways to [use it.]

Geometric shapes have been borro[wed] from patchwork quilts, and suns, [moons] and stars will always be popular m[otifs.] They are universal.

The beauty of country-style decora[tion is] the nonchalance with which motif[s,] styles and patterns can be mixed. [The] only decorative effect to be avoide[d is the] mass-produced adulterated version[s of] country-style designs, because the[y] have lost their heart and soul in th[e] manufacturing process!

LEFT: *Decorative surface detail is characteristic of country style, as in this free-hand painted box.*

RIGHT: *The heart, a perennial favourite, is appliquéd in a repeat pattern on this patchwork piece.*

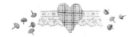

CLOCKWISE FROM TOP LEFT: *Stencilled details give this chair a look of pure country. Geometric patterns are always popular choices for textiles. The free-hand, organic design on this box is inspired by nature. A tin heart is decorated with punched geometric patterns.*

Painted Table

It is still possible, thank goodness, to find bargain tables in junk shops, and this one cost less than a tenth of the price of a new one. It is the sort of table that you can imagine standing in a country cottage parlour, covered with a lace-edged cloth and laden with tea-time treats. There is no guarantee that you will find a similar table, but any old table could be decorated in the same way.

Before you decorate your bargain, you may have to strip off the old paint or varnish and treat it for wood-worm, as we did. Any serious holes can be filled with wood-filler and then sanded and stained to match. The trick is to emphasize the good features and play down the bad. Old table-tops look more interesting than new ones and are well worth sanding, bleaching and staining. The stain on the table legs contrasts well with the red and green paint used on the table-top. The lining can be attem free-hand, but masking tape makes job much easier. Mark the position lightly in pencil so that all the line the same distance from the edge.

MATERIALS

*table
wood-stain in shade 'Dark
Jacobean Oak'
household paintbrush
emulsion paint in red and green
1 cm/½ in square-ended artist's
brush
masking tape
shellac
beeswax polish
soft clean cloth*

1

Prepare and treat the table as necessary. Use a rag to rub the wood-stain into the table legs, applying more as it is absorbed into the wood. The finish should be an even, almost black tone.

2

Paint the base of the table-top with red emulsion.

3

Measure 5 cm/2 in in from the edge of the table and place a strip of masking tape this distance in from each of the edges. Leave a 2 cm/¾ in gap and then place the next strips of tape to run parallel with the first set.

4

Fill in the strip between the tape wit green paint and leave to dry.

<hr>

5

Apply two coats of shellac to the table.

<hr>

6

Finish the table with a coat of beeswax polish, buffing it to a warm sheen with a soft clean cloth.

Painted Chest

Before the eighteenth century, throughout northern Europe and Scandinavia a country bride took her own decorated linen chest into her new home. The dowry chest would have been made by her father, lovingly carved and painted as a farewell gift to his daughter. Marriage customs accounted for many rural crafts, and the family took great pride in providing a handsome chest for a bride. This custom was continued among the first settlers in North America.

The chest used in this project is a mixture of Old- and New-World influences. The shape is English, but the painted decoration was inspired by an old American dowry chest. The pattern used on the chest is geometric, but the

paint finish is very loosely applied, to give a good contrast between two styles. You can use the pattern to decorate any blanket chest, old or new, and then give it an antique finish with tinted varnish.

The most time-consuming aspect i accurate drawing-up of the pattern shapes, but it is worth spending ti get the proportions right. The con and spotting has to be done quickl the effect is one of controlled chao

MATERIALS

blanket chest
shellac, if necessary
Crown Compatibles paint in shades 'Dusky Blue' and 'Regency Cream'
household paintbrushes
tracing paper
pair of compasses
ruler
acrylic varnish in shade 'Antique Pine'
graining comb
clean damp cloth

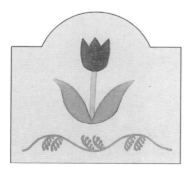

1

If you are starting with bare wood, apply a coat of shellac to seal the surface.

2

Paint the chest with Dusky Blue emu Trace and enlarge the pattern from template section and use it as a guic position the panels. Draw the panels a pair of compasses and ruler.

3

Fill in all the panels with cream emulsion.

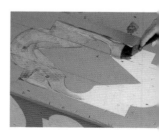

4

Apply a thick coat of varnish to o panel only.

5

ickly comb the varnish in a pattern,
wing the shape of the panel. Make one
oth combing movement into the wet
sh, and then wipe the comb to prevent
uild-up of varnish. Complete one panel
repeating steps 4 and 5 for the others.

6

y a coat of varnish to the whole chest.
mediately take a just-damp cloth,
it into a ball and use it to dab off spots
of the varnish.

Painted Bench

*Every home should have a bench like this, to squeeze extra guests around the
dinner table and to keep by the back door for comfortable boot-changing.
This bench was made by a carpenter, from a photograph seen in a book of
old country furniture. The wood is reclaimed floorboards, which give just the
right rustic feel to the bench.*

The decoration is applied in a rough
folk-art style that adds a touch of
humour. You can use this style to
decorate any bench, and even a plain
modern design will lose its hard edges
and take on the character of a piece of
rustic hand-made furniture.

MATERIALS

bench
medium-grade sandpaper
shellac
household paintbrushes
emulsion paint in deep red,

dark blue-grey and light
blue-green
small piece of sponge
varnish in shade 'Antique Pine'
clear matt varnish

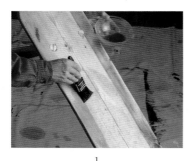

1

Sand the bare wood and seal it with a
coat of shellac.

2

Paint the legs in dark blue-grey emulsion,
working directly on to the wood.

3

Paint the seat with the
deep red emulsion.

4

Use the sponge to dab an even pattern of
blue-green spots across the whole surface of
the seat.

5

When the paint is dry, rub the seat and edges
with sandpaper, to simulate the wear and tear
of a thousand harvest suppers.

6

Apply one coat of Antique Pine varni[...]
the whole bench. Then apply two mor[...]
of matt varnish for a strong finish[...]

Shaker-inspired Peg Rail

*The Shakers were a religious movement whose ideals inspired a style of furnishings
and furniture of great simplicity and beauty of form. They did not believe in
ornamentation or decoration for its own sake, but held that functional objects
should be as beautiful and as well made as possible. The name 'Shaker' comes
from the ecstatic movements that occurred in their worship.*

Peg rails were very characteristic of
Shaker homes, and were used for hanging
all kinds of utensils and even chairs,
keeping the floor clear. Our rail is a very
inexpensive and simplified version of the
Shaker idea, and what it lacks in fine
craftsmanship it makes up for in
practicality. We have used a pine plank,
with a sawn-up broom-handle to make
the pegs. These rails work well all
around the house, but are especially
useful in hallways, children's rooms and
bathrooms. The coat of paint is not
strictly Shaker in style, but will disguise
the rail's humble origins.

MATERIALS

pine plank 2.5 cm l 1 in thick
ruler
saw
plane
drill with bit for broom-
handle holes
1 or 2 broom-handles
medium-grade sandpaper
wood glue

wooden block and hammer
shellac
household paintbrushes
Crown Compatibles emulsion
paint in shade 'Dusky Blue'
varnish in shade 'Antique Pine'
white spirit, if necessary
spirit-level
rawl plugs and long screw

1

Measure and cut the wood to the length
required. Plane it to smooth and
round the edges.

2

Mark the peg positions 20 cm/8 in
along the length. The spacing can be
to suit your requirements.

3

Drill holes 1.5 cm/⅗ in deep in which to
recess the pegs.

4

Cut up the broom-handles into 13 cm
lengths. Sand the edges to round the

5

wood glue and fit the pegs into their
es using a small wooden block and
hammer to fit them securely.

6

Apply one coat of shellac to seal the surface of
the wood.

7

Paint the rail blue.

8

edium-grade sandpaper to rub back to
bare wood along the edges.

9

Give the whole shelf a coat of Antique Pine
varnish. Dip a rag in white spirit (for
polyurethane varnish) or water (for acrylic
varnish) and rub off some of the varnish. Use
a spirit-level and ruler to mark the position of
the rail on the wall. Drill holes through the
rail at 40 cm/18 in intervals. Drill into the
wall, using suitable wall-fixings and screws.

Painted and Lined Country Chair

It is always worth buying interesting individual chairs when you spot them,
as they are often very inexpensive if they need 'doing up'. Four mismatching
chairs painted the same way will make a convincing and charming set,
and the effect is pure country.

This is a typical French, country-style, rush-seated chair, with curvaceous lines just begging to be accentuated with lining. The essentials of sturdiness and comfort have not been ignored, the seat is generously woven and it is very comfortable. (It is always worth sitting on your chair before you buy because it may have been custom-made for a differently shaped person!)

Colour is a real revitalizer and we have chosen a yellow and blue colour scheme reminiscent of the painter Monet's kitchen, to bring out the French character of the chair. It is worth spending time preparing the wood, and this may mean stripping all the paint if there are several layers of gloss. If you do have the chair professionally stripped, the joints will need to be re-glued, because the caustic stripper dissolves glue as well as paint.

MATERIALS

country-style chair
medium-grade sandpaper
undercoat
household paintbrushes
shellac and wood primer,
if necessary
Crown Satinwood paint in yellow
wire wool
hard pencil
tube of artist's oil colour in
ultramarine blue
white spirit
long-haired square-ended
artist's brush
varnish in shade 'Antique Pine

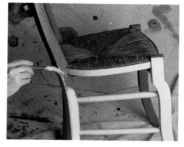

1

If the chair hasn't been stripped, rub it down well with medium-grade sandpaper. Apply the undercoat, or if the chair has been stripped, give it a coat of shellac followed by wood primer. Paint the chair yellow.

2

When this coat has dried, use wire wool to rub the paint back along the edges where natural wearing away would take place. With a pencil draw the lining, following the curves of the chair.

3

the oil paint with white spirit in the proportions 3 parts paint to 1 part white . You need paint that flows smoothly on the brush and allows you to retain control. If you find the paint too runny, more colour. Practise the brushstroke the artist's brush on scrap paper or d, supporting your brush-hand with spare hand. Controlling your lines is a er of confidence, which grows as you paint. Paint the lining on the legs, chairback and seat.

4

When dry, rub back with wire wool in places, as you did with the yellow.

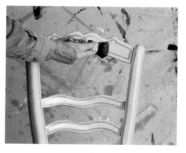

5

Finally apply a coat or two of varnish to soften the colour and protect the lining.

Pie-safe Cupboard

Cupboards like this one were mainly used in America as cooling cupboards for freshly baked goods. The doors were made out of decoratively punched and pierced tin sheets that allowed the delicious aromas to waft out, but prevented flies from getting in. They were called 'safes' because they were fitted with locks to keep temptation out of reach of little fingers lured by delicious smells!

We used an existing old pine cupboard to make the pie-safe, replacing the wooden front panels with newly pierced tin ones. Milled-steel sheet can be bought from sheet-metal suppliers, or try asking at a hardware store or looking in Yellow Pages. Care must be taken, as the edges of the sheet are very sharp, and need to be folded over to make a safe seam. You can crimp or flatten the edges using pliers.

The actual patterning is done with a hammer and nail, or, for more linear piercing, you can use a small chisel. This pattern is our own interpretation of a traditional design, but once you begin, your own style will emerge. You may find other ways of making patterns, perhaps using the end of a Phillips screwdriver, for instance – really anything goes. If the cupboard is to be used in the kitchen, add a protective backing sheet behind the tin, to cover the sharp edges. To get rid of the very new gleam of pierced metal, rub vinegar into the surface.

MATERIALS

old cupboard with one or two panelled doors
tracing paper
medium-grade sandpaper
shellac, if necessary
24- or 26-gauge milled-steel sheet(s) to fit (allow 1 cm / ½ in all around for the seams)
pliers and tinsnips, if necessary
masking tape

pair of compasses or transfer paper
chinagraph pencil
hammer
selection of different nails, screwdrivers and chisels
backing material such as hardboard, if necessary
panel pins
varnish in shade 'Antique Pine'
household paintbrush

1

Remove any beading and ease out the existing panels from the cupboard doors. Measure the space and use tracing paper to plan the design to fit. Rub down the cupboard with sandpaper. If it has been stripped, re-seal it with a coat of shellac. Trim the metal sheet, if necessary. Fold over the sharp edge of the metal sheet, to make a seam about 1 cm / ½ in deep around the edge. Crimp firmly with pliers. Put masking tape over sharp edges, to prevent accidental cuts.

2

Transfer your design on to the tin su[...] using a pair of compasses. If you find [...] tricky, trace the whole design and use t[...] paper to put it on to the metal. Add[...] extra designs with the chinagraph pe[...]

3

se piercing on a scrap of tin, such as a
t-tin lid, so that you know how hard
ed to hit the nail to pierce a hole, and
how just to dent the surface without
ng it. Place thick cardboard or an old
or blanket beneath the tin to absorb
se and protect the surface underneath.
you are confident with the hammer
ail, or whatever tool you want to use,
hammer out the pattern.

4

pierced panels, and the backing if you
sing it, into the door and replace the
g to secure it. Use short panel pins at
ance of 4 cm/1½ in apart, all around
the panel to fix in place.

5

andpaper the edges to simulate a
orn effect. Give the wood a protective
coat of antiquing varnish.

49

Shelf with Hanging Hooks

This large shelf with a backboard and hooks would suit a kitchen, entrance hall or large bathroom. It is really simple to make, requiring only the most basic of carpentry skills and tools. The shelf can be painted or varnished, depending on the wood, and it's a really handsome and useful piece of furniture.

The very best wood to use is reclaimed pine, usually floorboards. Demolition or builder's reclamation yards usually have stocks of old wood, but be prepared to pay more for old than new pine. If you're leaving the shelf unpainted it's definitely worth the extra money for old wood. If you intend to paint the shelf, new wood can be used for the backing board, to cut down on the price.

The best feature of the shelf is the very generously sized brackets, which were copied from an old farm storeroom. They have been cut from a section of old pine door, using a jig-saw. The brackets will support the shelf and balance the weight, but the shelf should be screwed into a sound brick wall, using suitable rawl plugs and long steel screws.

This type of shelf is very popular in rural eastern European communities. The hooks can either be new brass or wrought-iron coathooks; or you may be lucky enough to find an old set. Either way they are bound to be concealed, as hooks usually attract more than they were ever intended to hold!

MATERIALS

*tracing paper
piece of pine 34 cm × 18 cm ×
3 cm / 14½ in × 7 in × 1¼ in
thick, for the brackets
jig-saw
drill with No. 5 and 6 bits
pine plank 100 cm × 15 cm ×
2 cm / 3 ft 4 in × 6 in × ¾ in
thick, for the backboard
pine plank 130 cm × 22 cm ×
2 cm / 4 ft 4 in × 8½ in × ¾ in
thick, for the shelf
wood glue
wood-screws
shellac
household paintbrush
2.5 cm / 1 in brush
Crown Compatibles emulsion
paint in shades 'Dusky Blue',
'Aqua Spring', and 'Precious Jade'
clean damp cloth
wire wool
medium-grade sandpaper
6 coathooks
rawl plugs, if necessary
3 long screws*

1

Trace the bracket pattern from the tem section and enlarge it until the longes measures 33.5 cm / 13½ in. Trace this the wood, fitting it into one corner, an flip the pattern over and trace it again the opposite-end corner. The two ca cut out at the same time, using a jig Use the number 5 drill bit to make two through the backboard into the bracke also through the shelf down into t brackets. Spread wood glue on all the j edges, and then screw them togeth with wood-screws.

2

Apply one coat of shellac to the whole unit.

3

Use the 2.5 cm / 1 in brush to apply a c Dusky Blue emulsion.

4

en dry, apply a coat of Aqua Spring.

5

diately afterwards, use a damp cloth to
wipe the paint off in some areas.

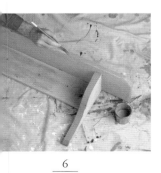

6

the edges of the shelf and brackets with
Precious Jade.

7

Rub away some of the dried paint using wire
wool. This will reveal the wood grain
along the edges.

8

Finally rub down with medium-grade
sandpaper to smooth the finish and reveal the
grain. Screw in the hooks. Attach to the wall
by drilling through the backboard to make
holes for long wood-screws. Use suitable
wall fixings, if necessary.

Painted Dresser

If there is one item of furniture that typifies country style in most people's minds, it must surely be the dresser. A sturdy base cupboard topped with china-laden shelves is an irresistible sight.

This dresser was made by a local carpenter using reclaimed pine, but a dresser can easily be made up using a sturdy chest of drawers combined with a set of bookshelves. The trick is to make sure that the two are balanced visually, with the height and depth of the shelves suiting the width of the base. You can join the two unobtrusively by using strong steel brackets at the back, and painting will complete the illusion that the two were made for each other.

The washed-out paint finish is achieved by using no undercoat and rubbing the dried paint back to the wood with sandpaper and wire wool. Alternatively you can rub some areas of the wood with candle wax before you begin painting; the candle wax will resist the paint, leaving the wood bare.

MATERIALS

dresser, or combination of shelves
and base cupboard
shellac
household paintbrushes
Crown Compatibles emulsion
paint in shades 'Dusky Blue',

'Quarry-tile Red' (optional) and
'Regency Cream'
household candle (optional)
medium-grade sandpaper and
wire wool
varnish in shade 'Antique Pine'

1

Apply a coat of shellac to seal the bare wood.

2

Paint the dresser Dusky Blue, followi[ng]
direction of the grain. Allow to d[ry]

3

If desired, rub candle wax along the edges
of the dresser before painting with a
second colour.

4

The wax will prevent the second colou[r]
adhering completely, and will crea[te a]
distressed effect. Add the second col[our]
if using.

5

t the backing boards Regency Cream,
n following the direction of the grain.

6

en the paint has dried, use medium-
sandpaper and wire wool to rub back
are wood along the edges, to simulate
wear and tear.

7

nally apply a coat of Antique Pine
varnish to the whole dresser to
protect the surface.

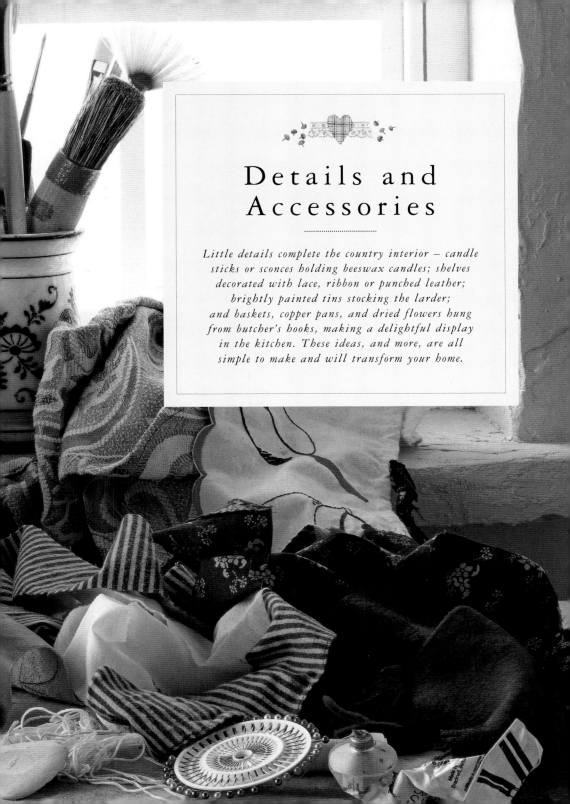

Details and Accessories

Little details complete the country interior – candle sticks or sconces holding beeswax candles; shelves decorated with lace, ribbon or punched leather; brightly painted tins stocking the larder; and baskets, copper pans, and dried flowers hung from butcher's hooks, making a delightful display in the kitchen. These ideas, and more, are all simple to make and will transform your home.

Finishing Touches

Once you have transformed your home with country-style paint finishes, furniture and flooring, it is time to add the finishing touches. The accumulation of 'finds' that add personality to a home does take time, and should be a gradual process; it often depends on your being in the right place at the right time. An unlimited supply of money would buy you folk-art treasures and an interior-designed country look, but you would certainly miss out on the pleasure of making your own accessories.

There are projects in this section to suit most talents and skills, whether your talent lies with a needle and thread, carpenter's tools or paintbrushes.

A simple broom-handle can be used to display a collection of baskets hanging from the ceiling and découpage transforms any ordinary tray into one to be displayed on the wall as 'art'.

Shelving can be dressed up with lace, ribbons, paper or even punched leather, to make something functional into a decorative feature. It is well worth seeking out a local carpenter if you lack

ABOVE: *This punched-tin sconce creates a wonderful backdrop for candles.*

the space or inclination to make your own shelving, because reclaimed timber like pine floorboarding is really worth using for its character and colour.

Candlelight is essential for adding a cosy atmosphere, and whether you choose to make the baluster candlesticks or the rustic wall sconce, you will be enriching the room with something unusual and hand-made. Use the ideas suggested as a starting point, adding your own colour schemes and patterns to give each thing you make a personal touch.

The embroidered pelmet looks very special, and the shapes do not require any particular needlecraft skill to follow. A simple chain stitch could be used to outline all the shapes, and satin stitch for the scallops. The more advanced embroiderer could elaborate upon the designs, filling the background as well as the kitchen implements with a variety of colours and fancy stitchwork.

Similarly, the patchwork throw do need any more than basic sewing-machine skills to fit it together. T design will vary, depending on you selection of warm winter scarves a backing fabric, and the more exper seamstress will be tempted to mak pattern more complicated by addi differently shaped patches. Wheth choose to make the basic throw or a complicated variation, you are bou be delighted with the result. It loo great draped over a chair and is marvellously warm and insulating cold country evening.

There are many country crafts that studied and mastered, like basket-making, weaving or the carving of ducks. If you have time to explore learn about how things are traditic made, it is very enriching. Our pro are more about taking short cuts a making an impact, which is a good creative starting point. Once you r the pleasure that is to be gained fr both making and displaying your creations, you are bound to continu experiment and to enjoy country c

LEFT AND RIGHT: *Beauty and practicality are the keynotes of any country kitchen. Utensils are displayed within easy reach, and dried goods may be kept in colourfully painted tins.*

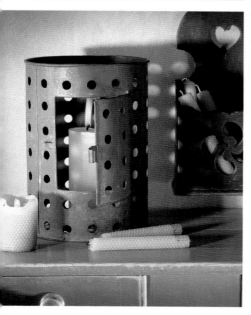

CLOCKWISE FROM TOP LEFT: *A painted salt box, Shaker-style doll and varnished trug all add a feeling of country. Candles complete the scene. Sewing odds and ends can be kept tidy in a wooden box. These whirligigs form an eye-catching still-life with a collection of plates in complementary colours. A colour-washed tin lantern sets off a display of beeswax candles.*

Wall Sconce

These fashionable room accessories were once essential to every household; however, one wonders what our ancestors would make of us forsaking the convenience of electricity for the 'romance' of candlelight. The truth is that technology and mass-production seem to take the humanity out of our homes, making us long for the irregularity of candlelight, hand-stitching and country-crafted furniture.

MATERIALS

old piece of wood
saw
hammer
brass and black upholstery tacks
wood glue
nails

1

Saw through the wood, making two sections to be joined at right angles. Begin the pattern by hammering the upholstery tacks in a central line; the pattern can then radiate from it.

2

Form arrows, diamonds and crosses, using the contrast between the brass and black tacks to enhance your design.

3

Apply a coating of wood glue to th edge of the base. Hammer fine nails the back into the base.

Découpage Tray

A good tray will be strong enough to carry the tea things and handsome enough to hang up as a decoration when not in use. This one has been découpaged with a selection of old engraving tools, but you could follow the method using any design you choose.

…page takes you back to childhood; … out and gluing is a favourite … of children between the ages …nd ten. The grown-up version …tly more sophisticated, but the …ains.

The secret of good découpage lies in accurate cutting and in putting on enough coats of varnish. Serious enthusiasts use 30 layers, rubbing back with fine sandpaper between the coats. The idea is to bring the background up

to the level of the applied decoration, and then to and further depth with more coats, possibly to include crackle glaze and antique varnish. The final result should be convincing to both eye and touch.

MATERIALS

tray
…nt Magic woodwash in shade 'Maize'
household paintbrush
fine-grade sandpaper
…hotocopied motifs to cut out
…rp-pointed scissors or scalpel
…wallpaper paste and brush
soft cloth
…w paintbrush for varnishing
clear satin varnish
crackle glaze (optional)
…ist's oil paint in raw umber

1

Prepare the tray by painting it with Maize as a base colour. When dry, rub the surface with fine-grade sandpaper.

2

Cut out your paper shapes carefully, moving the paper towards the scissors, or around on the cutting surface, so that you are always using the scissors or scalpel in the most comfortable and fluid way.

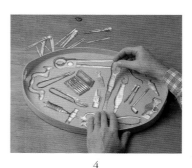

3

Turn the cut-outs over and paste the backs with wallpaper paste, right up to the edges, covering the whole area.

4

Stick them down in position on the tray.

. . . continued

5

Use a soft cloth to smooth out any bubbles.
Leave to dry overnight.

6

Begin varnishing, using a clean new brush
and applying a sparing coat to the whole
surface of the tray. When dry, rub lightly
with fine-grade sandpaper and repeat as many
times as possible.

7

A further dimension has been added
découpage, by the application of a c
glaze. There are several brands on
market. It is best to follow the spe
instructions for the product you
Here the base varnish is being pai
on to the tray.

8

When this coat is dry (after 20 minutes),
apply an even coat of crackle glaze and leave
it to dry for 20 minutes.

9

Rub a small amount of artist's oil paint into
the cracks, using a cotton cloth. Raw umber
was used here, which gives a naturally aged
effect but any colour can be used.

10

When the cracks have been colou
gently rub the excess paint from the
using a soft cloth.

11

Give the tray at least two more coats
satin varnish; many more if time
patience allow.

Wooden Candlesticks

This pair of matching wooden candlesticks have been made from old balusters that were removed from a stair rail. This is an easy way to make something from turned wood without having to operate a lathe yourself. Balusters can be bought singly from wood merchants or DIY stores.

The only special equipment needed is a vice and a flat-head drill bit, to make a hole in the top of the baluster large enough to hold a candle.

The candlesticks have been painted in bright earthy colours, giving a matching pair fit to grace any country table.

MATERIALS

saw
2 wooden balusters (reclaimed or new)
2 square wood off-cuts
medium- and fine-grade sandpaper
wood glue
vice

electric drill fitted with a flat-head drill bit
acrylic paint in bright yellow, re and raw umber or burnt sienna household and artist's brushes
clear matt acrylic varnish
soft clean cloth

1

Cut out the most interesting section of the baluster and a square base; this one measures 7.5 × 7.5 cm/3 × 3 in. Roughen the bottom of the baluster with sandpaper.

2

Very slightly, chamfer the base with fine-grade sandpaper. Glue the two sections together with wood glue.

3

Hold the candlestick securely in the drill a hole for the candle 2 cm/¾ diameter and 2 cm/¾ in deep

4

Paint with two or three coats of bright yellow acrylic paint.

5

Apply a coat of orange acrylic paint (add a touch of red to the yellow acrylic).

6

Tint the varnish to a muddy brow adding a squeeze of raw umber or sienna. Brush this over the oran

7

umpled cloth to lift some varnish and
reveal the colour below.

When using wooden candlesticks do not
leave burning candles unattended or allow
the candle to burn right down, as the wood
may catch fire.

Woollen Patchwork Throw

*Believe it or not, this stunning chair throw cost next to nothing to make, and was
finished in an afternoon! It is made from pure woollen scarves and remnant
wool fabric. The scarves come from charity shops, and can be bought for pennies.
You will be spoilt for choice, so choose a colour scheme derived from your remnant.
The throw is lined with a length of old brocade curtain, but a flannel sheet
would also be suitable, especially if you dyed it a dark colour.*

The only skill you need for this project is
the ability to sew a straight line on a
sewing machine: and tartan scarves
provide good guidelines to follow. Clear
a good space on the floor and lay the
fabric and scarves out, moving them
around until you are happy with the
colour combinations. Cut out the first
central square. The diamond shape will
need to be hemmed and tacked before
you sew it to the centre of the first
square; after this, each strip of scarf
will just need to be pinned and sewn
in position.

The throw could easily be adapted to
make a bedcover, and, because of the
fine-quality wool used for scarves, it will
be exceptionally warm. The challenge
with this throw is to resist draping
yourself in it, instead of the chair!

scissors
about 1 m / 1 yd wool fabric
selection of plaid and plain
woollen scarves
pins, thread and sewing machine
old curtain or flannel sheet,
for lining

1

a 46 × 46 cm / 18 × 18 in square of
ckground' fabric. Choose the pattern
r central diamond and cut a square,
ng the width of the scarf as the
rement for the sides. Turn the edges
cm / ½ in and tack. Pin and sew the
diamond in position.

2

Choose two scarves and cut them into four
rectangles. Position them along the sides of
the square, with the matching patterns
facing each other. Sew them in place and
trim off any excess.

3

four matching plain squares and pin
them into the corners. Check on the
side, to make sure that the corners
t accurately. Cut four strips of the
ckground fabric to fit the sides.

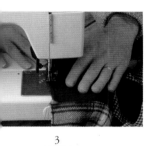

4

Cut out four corner pieces of the scarf used
for the central diamond, 14 cm × 14 cm /
5½ in × 5½ in. Sew a square to one end of
each strip of background fabric.

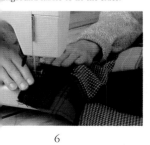

5

Pin and then sew these long strips in position
around the edge of the patchwork.

6

lain scarf into four strips lengthways
ew these around the outside edge,
apping at the corners to complete
the square.

7

Cut the lining to fit and sew the two pieces
together, with their right sides
facing inwards.

8

Turn inside out and sew up the seam by
hand. Press, using a damp cloth and
dry iron

Plaited 'Rag-rug' Tie-backs

Tie-backs are an attractive way of getting the maximum amount of daylight into the house. It is surprising how much difference a few inches more exposure of window panes can make to the light in a room, so unless your windows are huge, it is well worth tying your curtains back into the wall. This idea has a real hands-on feel and can be made to co-ordinate or contrast with existing curtains.

This method of plaiting scraps of fabric has been stolen from rag-rug makers, and if you have always wanted to make one, this may be just the introduction that you need! If you have any fabric left over from your curtains, you could incorporate this into the plaits. If not, one plain colour that appears in your curtaining will have a harmonizing effect on the whole scheme.

MATERIALS

*scraps of fabric cut into 7.5-cm/
3-in wide strips
safety pin
needle and thread
scissors
strip of fabric for backing (one for
each tie-back)
2 D-rings for each tie-back*

1

Roll up the fabric strips, leaving a we
length unfurled.

2

Join three strips together, rolling one fabric around the other two and pinning them together with the safety pin. Attach the ends to a chair or any suitable stationary object or anchor them under a heavy weight. Begin plaiting, rolling the strips into tubes as you go, so that the rough edges are turned in and concealed. Make tight plaits. The tie-back needs to be at least 50 cm/20in long and four plaits deep.

3

Work until you have the required length and number of plaits. Lay the plaits flat and sew the edges together using a large needle and strong thread pulled up tight. Keep the plaits flat when you turn at either end.

4

Cut a backing strip, allowing enough
to turn under 1.5 cm/⅝in all round.
the D-rings at either end as you slip
the lining into place.

Quilted Tie-backs

This is a quilting project for the absolute beginner. All that is required is the ability to sew an even running stitch along a drawn line. The pattern is a standard quilting stencil (available from craft shops), which you draw through using a chalky coloured pencil. A layer of wadding is placed between two strips of fabric, which can then be tacked or pinned together.

The effect produced by the quilting is textural and the pattern shows up very well. The quilting is best done on plain fabrics, like the calico we used, but the tie-backs could be used with patterned curtains. Gingham or larger checked patterns look especially good teamed with quilted calico.

MATERIALS

1 m / 1 yd unbleached calico
scissors
50 cm / 20 in quilter's wadding
quilt stencil pattern
chalky coloured pencil
pins, needle and thread
2 D-rings for each tie-back

1

Cut the calico into strips 50 cm × 14 cm/ 20in × 5¾ in. Cut the wadding into strips 48cm × 10 cm/19in × 4 in. Use the stencil to draw on to one piece of calico.
Put a layer of wadding in between two layers of calico and pin.

2

Sew a running stitch along the pattern lines. You may find it easiest to pull the needle through each time, rather than sewing in and out of all three layers at once.

3

When the pattern is complete, fold edges and stitch them all around, e by hand or machine. Attach a D-r at each end.

Leather-edged Shelf Trimming

Not all shelves are worthy of display, especially the new and inexpensive ones that are readily available in DIY stores. There is no denying that they are practical and functional, and a simple shelf trimming will transform them very quickly into a charming and individual room feature.

MATERIALS

*...ther off-cuts (sold by weight
in craft shops)
...und template with a 7.5 cm /
3 in diameter
pencil, ruler and chalk
pinking shears
multi-sized hole punch
double-sided tape or glue*

1

...ips of leather to fit the length of your
...sing several sections to make up the
... if necessary. The edging needs to be
...2½ in deep. Draw a line 1 cm /½ in
...he edge (on the reverse side) and use
...mplate to draw semi-circles along the
length of the line.

2

...und these with pinking shears. Punch
...es around the edges, varying the sizes.

3

Draw stars on the semi-circles with chalk.
Punch out holes around the star outlines in
the same way. Run a strip of double-sided
tape along the shelf, and use this to attach
the leather trim; alternatively all-purpose
glue can be used.

Lace and Gingham Shelf Trimming

The lacy look may not suit every room, but it can add a very French touch to a dresser or kitchen shelf. The contrast between stout enamel pans and fine cotton lace can be quite charming; in French country homes, crochet lace is pinned up for display on any shelf available.

There are so many different lace designs available, that the decision will have to be a personal one. You may go for an antique hand-crocheted piece or a simpler machine-made design. The pointed edging chosen here suits a china display very well.

There is something both cheerful and practical about gingham. It is perfectly suited to edging food-cupboard shelves, where the pattern is strong enough to stand out against all the different packaging designs. The combination with lace is fresh and pretty.

MATERIALS

strips of lace the length of the
cupboard shelves, plus extra for
turnings
cold tea
small bowl

scissors
double-sided tape
gingham ribbon the length of the
sides of the shelves
all-purpose glue

1

To tone down the brightness of this new lace, it was dipped into a bowl of cold tea. The stronger the brew, the darker the colour, so adjust it by adding water to lighten the dye, if necessary. Press the lace when dry and cut it to the correct length.

2

Apply the double-sided tape to the v[...] sides of the shelves and peel off the b[...] tape. Cut the gingham ribbon to fit [...] seal the ends with a little glue, which will dry clear and preven[...] the ends from fraying.

3

Stick the gingham ribbon to the verticals, carefully smoothing it out and keeping it straight. Start at one end, and keep the ribbon taut.

4

Apply double-sided tape to the edges of the shelves, overlapping the gingham.

5

Seal one end of the lace with a small a[...] of glue. Stretch it along the tap[...] cut it to fit and seal the edge. Repe[...] the other shelves.

French Bread Bin

The kitchen and meal-times play a central role in country life, entailing warm winter suppers when the nights have drawn in, or long, languorous lunches in the height of summer. Crusty bread is an integral part of any meal, and this stylish bread bin will bring a touch of French country style to your kitchen. The same design could be used in a hallway or by the back door to hold umbrellas or walking sticks.

The pattern provided in the template section could be given to a carpenter, or, if woodworking is a hobby, made at home. The stand has been made from reclaimed pine floorboards, which are quite heavy and give it stability, as does the moulding used to broaden the base.

The decoration is called ferning and was very popular in Victorian times. Dried or imitation ferns (florists sell fake plastic or silk ones) are sprayed with aerosol mounting adhesive and arranged on the surface, which is then spray-painted. It dries very quickly and the ferns can then be lifted off. The effect is stunning and very easy to achieve.

MATERIALS

wood for the stand (see pattern)
tracing paper or transfer paper
jig-saw or coping saw
wood glue and 2.5 cm / 1 in
panel pins
hammer

For the decoration
shellac
household paintbrush
newspaper
masking tape
spray adhesive
selection of artificial ferns
spray-paint in black, dark green
or dark blue
fine-grade sandpaper
clear matt varnish

1

Apply two coats of shellac to seal and the bare wood.

TO MAKE THE STAND

Cut the timber to the dimensions shown on the pattern in the template section. Mitre the edges. Trace the pattern for the back detail and cut it out using a jig-saw or coping saw. Apply wood glue to all joining edges, join them and then use panel pins to secure them.

2

Working on one side at a time, mask off the surrounding area with newspaper and masking tape. Apply mounting spray to one side of the ferns and arrange them on the surface.

3

Spray on the colour, using light, even and building up the colour gradua. Lift the ferns when the paint is dr

4

rk on all the sides and the inside back
panel in the same way.

5

the edges to simulate a time-worn look.

6

Finally, apply two coats of varnish
to protect the fernwork.

Rabbit Dummy Board

A free-standing oversized rabbit will certainly provide both a focal and a talking point! Dummy boards originated as shop or inn signs; in the days when few people could read, a painted sign would indicate the trade being practised on the premises. The signs would either hang above the doorway or stand on a wooden block. You can give this rabbit a support to make it stand up, or hang it on the wall.

This project employs a mixture of old and new, as it is an original nineteenth-century engraving enlarged on a photocopier. The fine lines of the original thicken up with enlargement, but not enough to lose the effect of an engraving.

This project is great fun and fairly simple, and the only real skill required is that of cutting the shape out with a jig-saw. Personal experience has shown us that there are people who delight in this; so if you don't have a jig-saw – find someone who does!

MATERIALS

wallpaper paste and brush
A2 (59.5 × 42 cm/
23¼ × 16¼ in) sheet of marine
plywood (or similar)
jig-saw
fine-grade sandpaper
shellac
household paintbrushes
varnish in shade 'Antique Pine'
clear matt varnish
scrap of wood for stand
PVA glue

3

Apply a coat of wallpaper paste to the plywood. This seals the surface and provides a key for the pasted paper.

1

Photocopy the rabbit pattern from the template section, enlarging it to the edges of an A4 sheet. Cut the enlargement in half to give two A5 sheets.

2

Enlarge both of these up to A3 siz Depending on the machine, this pro can be done in one step, or might t several enlargements.

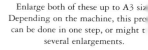

4

Trim the 'joining' edges of the photoc right up to the print, so that they can b against each other with no overlap. Ap thin layer of wallpaper paste right up edges and stick the two halves togeth the board. Smooth out any bubbles w soft cloth and leave it to dry overnig

5

a jig-saw to cut out the shape, leaving a
ase. Using a jig-saw is not difficult, but
will need to practise to get the feel of it.
Take your time.

6

and the edges of the rabbit smooth.

7

he surface with a coat of shellac, which
ive it a yellowish glow. Apply a coat of
que Pine varnish, followed by several
coats of clear varnish.

8

Trace the pattern from the template section.
Use it to cut out the stand. Rub down the
edges with fine sandpaper and glue in place.

Painted Tin or Tôleware

Tin-painting reached its zenith in the early days of American settlement, when itinerant merchants would appear in a blaze of colour at farm gates, selling their decorated tin housewares. Even then, they were hard to resist and most homes boasted a display of painted tinware. The word 'tôleware' derives from the French tôle peinte *meaning 'painted tin', but the style of painting owes more to the Norwegian* rosemaling *than the elaborate French style.*

Our project does not require you to learn the specialized brushstrokes used in traditional tin-painting, although the colours and antiquing will ensure that it blends in well with any other tôleware pieces. These numbered tins were used by tea merchants as containers for different tea blends.

MATERIALS

metal primer
household paintbrushes
large metal tin (either tin or
aluminium) with a lid
emulsion paint in black,
brick-red and maize-yellow
selection of artist's brushes
tracing paper (optional)
soft pencil
masking tape
hard pencil
shellac
clear varnish tinted with
raw umber acrylic paint
clear satin varnish

_1_

...he the tin. Paint the lid with black
...ion and the tin brick-red, with bands
of maize-yellow.

_2_

Trace or photocopy the pattern from the
template section and then cross-hatch over
the back with a soft pencil.

_3_

...low-tack masking tape to hold the
...rn in position and then draw over it
...a hard pencil, transferring an outline
to the tin.

_4_

Fill in the main body of the '3'
in maize-yellow.

_5_

Fill in the shadow in black.

_6_

...nish the tin with shellac to give it
a warm glow.

_7_

Apply a coat of tinted varnish and then
give it a coat of clear satin varnish
to protect the surface.

Curtain-pole Hanging Display

The Victorian clothes airer made use of the warmth above the range in the days before tumble driers. These days they are seldom used for their original purpose; instead they are adorned with hooks that hold copper pans, baskets and other delights.

However, not all ceilings are suitable for a heavy airer, and some are not high enough for a hanging display of this sort. For the country look without the creaking timbers and bumped heads, try this attractive, painted curtain pole.

The wooden curtain poles used here can be bought from any DIY store.

MATERIALS

curtain pole, plus turned finials
(not brackets)
2 large 'eye' bolts for ceiling beam
medium-grade sandpaper
emulsion paint in green, red and
cream

household paintbrushes
clear varnish tinted with ra
nmber acrylic paint
2 equal lengths of chain
cup hooks and butcher's hook
for displays

1

Using the pole as a measuring guide, position and screw into the ceiling or beam the two 'eye' bolts. These must be very sturdy and firmly fixed. Sand down the pole and finials, and then paint the finials green.

2

Paint the pole red. When the pole is dry, paint the cream stripes 6 cm / 2½ in from the ends.

3

Sand the paint in places to give an age
Fit the finials on the ends of the pole.
a coat of tinted varnish. Attach the le
of chain to the 'eye' bolts. Screw in tw
hooks to the pole in the correct posit
line up with the bolts. Attach the bu
hooks for hanging your decoratio
hang up the pole and add your disp

Embroidered Pelmet

In France, pelmets such as this one are often pinned up above windows
that do not need curtains, but that would otherwise be too plain.

nbroidery is simply made from a
sic stitches and is quite suitable
eginner to attempt. Gingham
ns provide a simple contrast
it detracting from the embroidered
n, but you could make calico
ns and embroider them with the
lesigns – if you have time and have
under the embroidery spell!

MATERIALS

tracing paper
dressmaker's transfer paper or
carbon pencil
1 m / 1 yd calico, cut into
2 strips 20 cm / 8 in deep
needle and embroidery threaa
in 4 colours
scissors
curtain wire

1

Enlarge the patterns from the template
section to approximately 10 cm / 4 in.
Use transfer paper or carbon pencil to
transfer the patterns on to the calico.

2

Depending on your knowledge and level of
skill, embroider each of the designs.
A simple chain-stitch can be used, but
cross-stitch, stem-stitch, back-stitch and
French knots will add variety.

3

Use satin-stitch to make the scalloped edge.
Carefully trim the edge. Sew a seam along
the top edge and thread a length of curtain
wire through it. Gather to fit the window.

Trompe-l'oeil Dhurrie

Canvas Floor Cloth

Stencilled Border

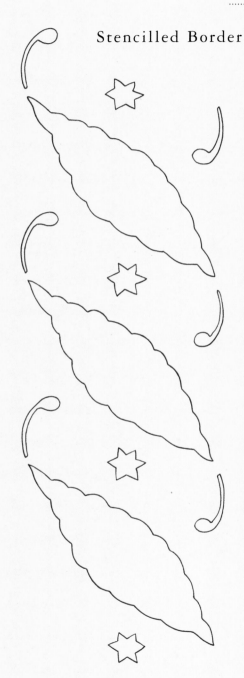
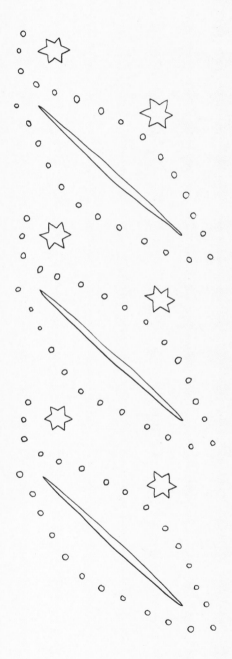

am-block Painting

Acorn and
Oak Leaf Border

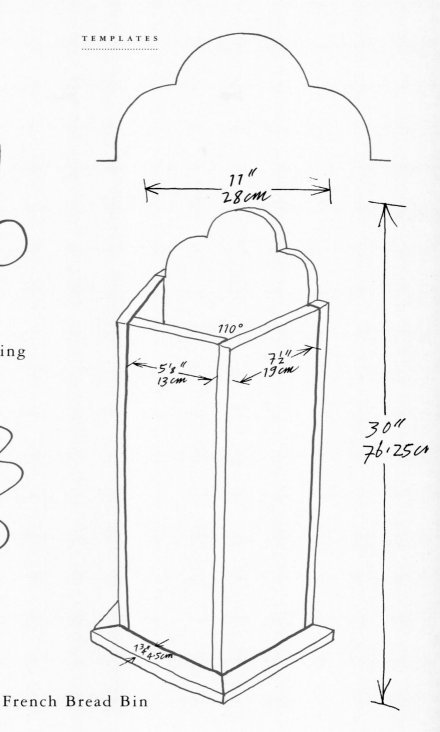

11″
28cm

110°

5⅛″
13cm

7½″
19cm

30″
76·25cn

1¾″
4·5cm

French Bread Bin

Painted Chest

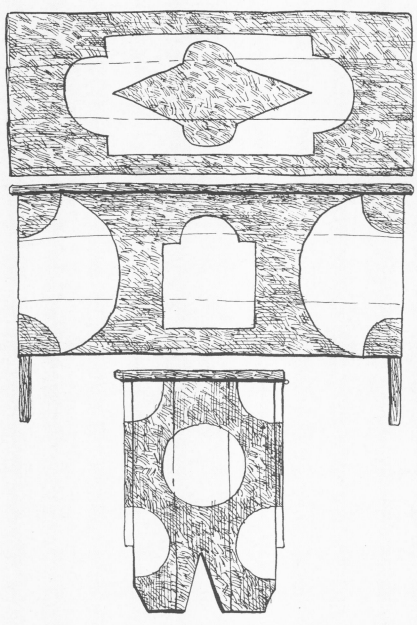

Rabbit Dummy Board

Shelf Bracket and Dummy Board Stand

Painted Tin Ware

Embroidered Pelmet

COUNTRY
Crafts and
Flowers

TESSA EVELEGH

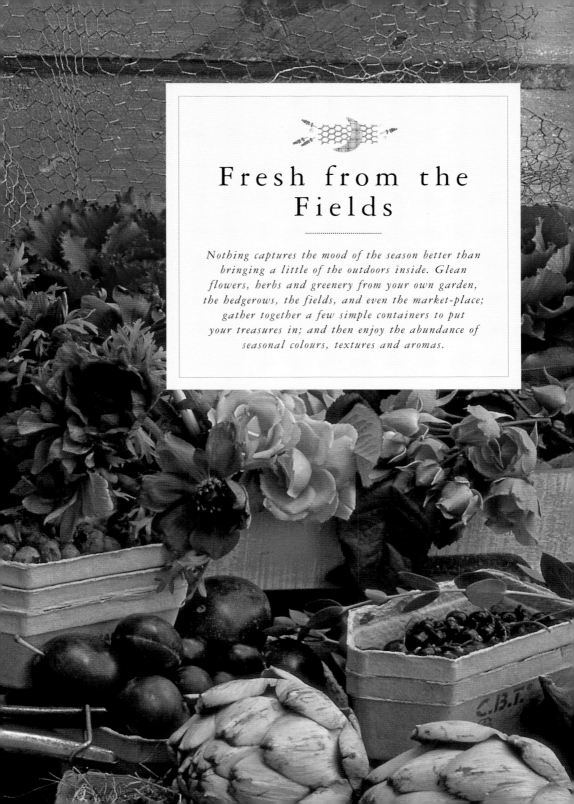

Fresh from the Fields

Nothing captures the mood of the season better than bringing a little of the outdoors inside. Glean flowers, herbs and greenery from your own garden, the hedgerows, the fields, and even the market-place; gather together a few simple containers to put your treasures in; and then enjoy the abundance of seasonal colours, textures and aromas.

Fresh Herb Wreath

Gather together a basketful of sweet fresh herbs and make them into an aromatic wreath, to hang in the kitchen or to use as a decorative garland for a celebration. If you choose the fleshier herbs — which hold their moisture — and spray the wreath well, it should last for a couple of days; after this you may wish to dismantle it and dry the individual bunches of herbs.

MATERIALS

florist's wire
scissors
fresh sage
fresh or dried lavender
fresh parsley
hot glue gun and glue sticks
wreath base, about 30 cm / 12 in in diameter
fresh chives
raffia

1

Using florist's wire, bind the sage, lavender and parsley into generous bunches.

2

Using the glue gun, fix two bunches to the wreath base, stems pointing in

3

Next, attach enough lavender bunches side by side to cover the width of the wreath base, hiding the sage stems. Attach bunches of parsley to cover the lavender stems in the same way.

4

Continue around the wreath base in this way, alternating the herbs, until it is generously covered.

5

Wire the chives into four generous b and trim the cut ends straight. Form pair into a cross and bind it with ra Wire the two chive crosses into posi

6

Tie raffia around the wreath at inte Make a raffia hanging loop, thread t to a generous bundle of raffia at the top of the wreath, and tie the ends o bundle into a bow.

Provençal Herb Hanging

Fix bunches of fresh herbs to a thick plaited rope, add tiny terracotta pots to give the design structure and then fill it in with garlic and colourful chillies to make a spicy, herbal gift full of Provençal flavour, for anyone who loves to cook.

MATERIALS

hank of seagrass string
scissors
garden string
florist's wire
fresh sage
fresh thyme
fresh oregano
2 small flowerpots
6 florist's stub wires
2 garlic heads
hot glue gun and glue sticks (optional)
large dried red chillies

1

Cut six lengths of seagrass string abou
times as long as the desired finished le
the hanging. Take two lengths, fold th
half and place them under a length of
string. Pass the cut ends over the stri
through the loop of the fold, there
knotting the seagrass on to the garden
  Repeat twice with the remaining f
seagrass lengths. Divide the seagrass
three bundles of four lengths and plai
to form the base of the herb hangi

2

Finish the end of the plait by binding it with a separate piece of seagrass string.

3

Using florist's wire, bind the herbs into small bundles and tie each one with garden string. Use this to tie them to the plaited base.

4

Wire the flowerpots by passing two wires through the central hole and tw the ends together.

5

Wire the pots to the base by passing a stub wire through the wires on the pots, passing it through the plait, and then twisting the ends together.

6

Tie garden string around the garlic and tie these to the base. Wire or the chillies into position, and fill the with more chillies.

Fresh-flower Fruit Bowl

Make the prettiest summer fruit bowl by arranging trailing flowers and foliage through a wire basket, topping it with chicken-wire and a pretty plate, and then piling on the fresh fruit. This is a delightful touch for outdoor entertaining.

MATERIALS

jam jar
wire basket
fuchsia flowers or
similar trailing blooms
secateurs
chicken-wire to fit the diameter
of the basket
attractive plate to fit the
diameter of the basket
selection of colourful fruit

1

Fill the jam jar with water and place it in the centre of the basket.

2

Trim the flower stems with secat and arrange them all round the ba by threading the stems through th and into the jar of water. Continue the flowers and foliage provide a d curtain of colour around the bas

3

Cut the chicken-wire to fit over the and fix it by bending it around the Place a plate on this chicken-wire, a fill the plate with colourful summer

Vegetable Centrepiece

*The flower stall is not the only source of material for centrepieces – the
vegetable stall provides great pickings, too. Here, a still-life of ornamental
cabbages – complemented by a simple cut-open red cabbage and some artichokes –
makes a flamboyant focal-point for the table. The theme is carried through by
adding an ornamental cabbage leaf to the cutlery bundle at each setting.*

MATERIALS

*dyed raffia
painted wooden basket
2 ornamental cabbages in pots
lichen moss
1 set of cutlery and napkin
per person
baby-food jar
painted trug
red cabbage, halved
globe artichokes*

| 1 | 2 | 3 |

bow of dyed raffia around the handle
the wooden basket. Remove several
erfect cabbage leaves and place the
bbages in their pots in the basket.

Cover the tops of the pots with silvery-grey
lichen moss.

Tie up each cutlery bundle with a napkin
and an ornamental cabbage leaf. Finish the
arrangement by putting a few more leaves
into a baby-food jar and tying dyed raffia
around it. Fill a garden trug with the red
cabbage halves and the globe artichokes.

Candle Centrepiece

Even the humblest materials can be put together to make an elegant centrepiece.
The garden shed has been raided for this one, which is made from a terracotta
flowerpot and chicken wire. Fill it up with red berries, ivies and white roses
for a rich, Christmassy look; or substitute seasonal flowers and foliage
at any other time of the year.

MATERIALS

18 cm / 7 in flowerpot
about 1 m / 39 in chicken wire
knife
florist's foam ball to fit the
diameter of the flowerpot

beeswax candle
tree ivy
white roses
berries
variegated trailing ivy

1

Place the pot in the centre of a large square
of chicken wire. Bring the chicken wire up
around the pot and bend it into position.

2

Cut the florist's foam ball in half and soak
one half. Reserve the other half for
another project.

3

Place the foam in the pot, cut-side up
have a flat surface. Position the candle
centre of the pot.

4

Arrange glossy tree-ivy leaves all around the
candle, to provide a lush green base.

5

Add a white rose as a focal point, and
bunches of red berries among the ivy.

6

Add more white roses, and intersp
trailing variegated ivy among the tre

Wild at Heart

Often, the simplest arrangements are the most appealing. Here, flowers are arranged very simply in little glass jars wound around with blue twine and carefully grouped to make a delightful still life.

MATERIALS

blue twine	scabious
2 jam jars	anemones
garden shears	glass plate

1

Wrap the blue twine around the jars and tie securely. Fill the jars with water.

2

Fill one jar with scabious and another with anemones, cutting the stems to the right lengths as you go.

3

Fill the plate with water.

4

Cut one of the flower stems very shor[t] allow the bloom to float in the plate. a delightful solution for any heads of that have broken off during trans[it]

Advent Candle Ring

An Advent candle ring makes a pretty Christmas centrepiece. This one – decorated with glossy tree ivy, delicate Cape gooseberries, dried citrus-fruit slices and bundles of cinnamon sticks – is not only a delight to the eye but also contributes a rich seasonal aroma.

MATERIALS

*florist's foam
knife
florist's ring basket
4 church candles
moss
dried orange slices
florist's stub wires
secateurs
cinnamon sticks
golden twine
tree ivy
Cape gooseberries*

1

Soak the florist's foam and cut it to fit the ring basket.

2

Position the candles in the foam

3

Cover the florist's foam with moss, pushing it well down at the sides of the basket.

4

Wire the orange slices by passing a stub wire through the centre and then twisting the ends together at the outside edge. Wire the cinnamon sticks into bundles, tie them with golden twine and then pass a wire through the twine.

5

Wire the tree-ivy leaves into bund

6

Position the ivy leaves in the ring. Decorate by fixing in the orange slices and cinnamon sticks. To finish, place the Cape gooseberries on top of the candle ring at intervals.

Autumn Fruitfulness

The sheer beauty of autumn produce makes it difficult to resist. It's too good to be left in the larder. Gather together all the softly bloomed purple fruits and pile them into a rich seasonal display for a side table or centrepiece.

MATERIALS

*metal urn
filling material, such as
bubble-wrap, newspaper or
florist's foam
several varieties of plums
black grapes
hydrangea heads
globe artichokes
blueberries*

1

Unless you have a huge abundance of fruit, fill the bottom of the urn with bubble-wrap, newspaper or florist's foam.

2

Arrange as many different varieties of as you can find on the filling, saving for the final decoration.

3

Add a large bunch of black grapes, d them over the rim of the urn. Finis arrangement with hydrangea head artichokes, scattered plums and blueb

Autumn Gold

The golds of autumn can be gathered into a fabulous display, using even the humblest of containers. Here, the dahlias have simply been put into a store-cupboard Kilner jar and given a seasonal necklace of hazelnuts.

MATERIALS

hazelnuts
seagrass string
secaturs
dahlias
Kilner jar
pumpkins
branches of pyracantha
with berries

1	2	3
he hazelnuts on to the seagrass string to make a 'necklace'.	Cut about 1 cm / ½ in off the end of each dahlia stem and place the stems in the Kilner jar filled with water.	Tie the hazelnut 'necklace' around the jar. Finish the arrangement with pumpkins and pyracantha branches.

Springtime Garland

Garlands of fresh flowers make delightful decorations for any celebration.
This pretty little hanging of pansies and violas has a woodland feel that
can be re-created at any time, because these flowers are available in
most months of the year.

MATERIALS

secateurs
chicken-wire the desired length of
the garland and three times the
desired width
scissors
black plastic bin liner
about two pansy plants for every
15 cm / 6 in of garland
about six viola plants for every
15 cm / 6 in of garland
florist's stub wires
moss

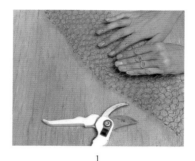

1

Using secateurs, cut the chicken-wire to size
and then form it into a flattened roll.

2

Cut the bin liner into squares large e
to cover the rootballs of the pans
and violas.

3

One by one, unpot each plant, gently r
any loose soil and place the rootball
the centre of a square of bin liner

4

Gather the plastic around the rootball and
fix it in place by winding stub wires loosely
round the top, leaving a short length free
to fix to the garland.

5

Fix the bagged-up plants to the garland
using the free end of wire.

6

Finish off by covering any visible plastic with
moss, fixing it with short lengths of florist's
stub wire bent hairpin-style.

Summer Gift Basket

Fresh flowers are always a welcome gift — make them into something extra special by laying them in a basket with prettily packaged, home-made strawberry jam.

MATERIALS

jar of strawberry jam
pink paper
glue
paper strawberry print
scissors
glazed pink paper
raffia
wooden basket
coloured paper
roses

1

Make up the pretty presentation for the strawberry jam by wrapping the jar with pink paper and gluing on a paper strawberry print to fix the paper.

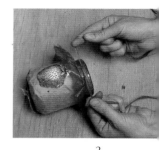

2

Make a top of glazed pink paper and tie. Line the basket with coloured pap fill it with a bunch of roses, tied with and the strawberry jam.

Christmas Gift Basket

Decorate a willow basket with gilded ivy leaves, and then pack it with seasonal goodies: a pot of variegated ivies and berries, decorative florist's pineapples, plus a few extra treats such as beeswax candles and crystallized fruits.

MATERIALS

tree ivy
picture framer's wax gilt
willow basket
scissors
hessian
pot of variegated ivy with berries
presents

1

Gild the tree ivy by rubbing on picture framer's wax gilt, using your fingers. Decorate the rim of the basket with these gilded leaves.

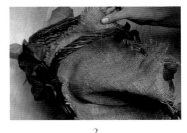

2

Cut a piece of hessian to size and fray the edges. Use the hessian to line the basket. Add the pot of ivy, plus presents to fill the basket.

Twiggy Door Wreath

Welcome seasonal guests with a door wreath that's charming in its simplicity.
Just bend a few twigs into a heart shape and adorn it with variegated ivy,
glowing berries and a pure-white rose.

MATERIALS

secateurs
pliable woody stems, such as buddleia,
cut from the garden
florist's wire
seagrass string
variegated trailing ivy
red berries
tree ivy
picture framer's wax gilt (optional)
white rose
golden twine

1

Using secateurs, cut six lengths of pliable
twigs about 70 cm / 28 in long. Wire three
together at one end. Repeat with the
other three. Cross the two bundles over
at the wired end.

2

Wire the bunches together in the
crossed-over position.

3

Holding the crossed, wired ends with one
hand, ease the long end round and down
very gently, so the twigs don't snap. Repeat
with the other side, to form a heart shape.
Wire the bottom end of the heart.

4

Cover the wiring by binding it with
seagrass string at the top and bottom
and make a hanging loop at the top.

5

Entwine strands of trailing ivy delicately
around the heart shape.

6

Add berries. Make a posy of tree-ivy leaves
(if you like, gild them using picture framer's
wax gilt) and a white rose. Tie the posy with
golden twine. Wire the posy in position at
the top of the heart.

Tied Posy

Flowers are at their most appealing when kept simple. Just gather together some garden cuttings and arrange them in a pretty posy that the recipient can simply unwrap and put straight into a vase, without further ado.

MATERIALS

secateurs   scabious
roses   brown paper
eucalyptus   ribbon

1

Using secateurs, cut each flower stem to approximately 15 cm/6 in long.

2

Gather the flowers together, surrounding each rose with some feathery eucalyptus, and then adding the scabious.

3

Wrap the posy with paper and tie with a pretty ribbon bow.

·····················

Tussie Mussie

Traditionally, tussie mussies were bouquets of concentrically arranged aromatic herbs that were carried around as a personal perfume. This one combines the blue-greens of sage and thyme with the soft blues of lavender and scabious flowers.

MATERIALS

6 scabious
fresh thyme
fresh lavender
fresh sage
dyed raffia

1

Encircle the scabious blooms
with fresh thyme.

2

Arrange a circle of lavender around this,
making sure the piece keeps its circular shape.

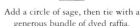

3

Add a circle of sage, then tie with a
generous bundle of dyed raffia.

Easter Display

Coloured eggs will immediately transform spring flowers into an Easter display.
Simplicity is the secret: just gather together an abundance of flowers and add
a few eggs, carefully laid on moss to evoke the idea of a nest.

MATERIALS

hard-boiled eggs
paper towels
food colouring (if the eggs are to be
eaten) or cold-water fabric dye
one glass jar for each colour
vinegar
salt
tulips or other spring flowers
secateurs
vase
moss
plate

1

Rinse the eggs in cold water. To mix the
dye, pour half a small bottle of food
colouring or put half a disc of fabric dye
into a glass jar, then pour on 300 ml/
½ pint/1¼ cups hot water.

2

Add 30 ml/2 tbsp vinegar and 15 ml/
1 tbsp salt. Lower an egg into the jar
of dye and leave it for a few minutes.
Check the colour regularly.

3

When the egg has reached the desired
colour, lift it out and repeat with the rest.
You will notice that the more eggs you
dye, the weaker the solution will become,
so each egg will need to be left in longer
to achieve the same effect. Cut about
1 cm/½ in off the end of each flower
stem and place them in a vase. Arrange
the coloured eggs on a nest of
moss on a plate.

Everlasting Treats

*Nature offers many exquisite textures and colours
that have natural everlasting qualities — or
that can be encouraged to have them — so scour the
countryside, dried-flower stockists, and even
your own store-cupboard for flowers, leaves, grasses
and dried whole spices; collect richly textured
strings, raffias and twines; and then transform
them into delightfully lasting natural gifts.*

Lavender Basket

A basket decorated with bunches of dried lavender makes an exquisitely pretty aromatic linen store. It could also be kept on the kitchen dresser, filled with freshly laundered tea towels ready on hand when you need them.

MATERIALS

dried lavender (2 bunches for the handle plus about 1 bunch for every 10 cm/4 in of basket rim)

florist's wire
scissors
willow basket

hot glue gun and glue sticks
blue paper-ribbon
blue twine

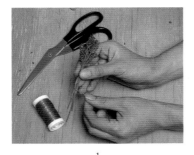

1

Wire up enough small bundles of about six lavender heads to cover the rim of the basket generously. Arrange the heads so they are staggered to give fuller cover. Trim the stalks short.

2

Wire up the remaining lavender into 12 larger bunches of about 12 lavender heads for the handles, leaving the stalks long.

3

Form a 'star' of three of the larger bun and wire them together. Repeat with other nine so you have four largish s shaped bunches of lavender.

4

Fix the small bunches to the rim of the basket, using either wire or hot glue in a glue gun. Start at one end and work towards the handle. Use the bunches generously so they overlap each other to cover the width of the rim.

5

Once the rim is fully covered, glue on individual heads of lavender to cover any spaces, ugly wires or stalks. Pay particular attention to the area near the handles, because you will have finished up with quite a few bare stalks there.

6

Wind blue paper-ribbon around the h Wire the longer lavender bunches to handles, leaving the stalks long b trimming to neaten them. Cut the sta the inside of the handle shorter to fi space. Bind the wired joints with blue

Heart of Wheat

Fashion a heart at harvest time, when wheat is plentiful, for a delightful decoration that would look good adorning a kitchen wall or dresser at any time of year. Despite its feathery looks, this heart is quite robust and should last for many years.

MATERIALS

*scissors
heavy-gauge garden wire or similar
florist's tape
silver reel wire
large bundle of wheat ears*

1

Cut three long lengths of heavy-gauge wire and bend them into a heart shape. Twist the ends together at the bottom.

2

Use florist's tape to bind the wire heart shape.

3

Using silver reel wire, bind together enough small bunches of wheat to cover the heart shape densely. Leave a short length of silver reel wire at each end for fixing to the heart shape.

4

Starting at the bottom, tape the first bunch of wheat ears to the heart.

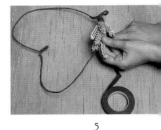

5

Place the second bunch further up the shape, behind the first, and tape it i position. Continue to tape the bunc until the whole heart is covered.

6

For the bottom, wire together about bunches of wheat ears, twist the wi together and wire them to the hea finishing off with florist's tape to nea This is what the back should look by the time you've finished.

Flower Topiary

Dried flowers look fabulous when given the sculptural form of faux *topiary.
These strawflowers and larkspur set into a tall cone make a stunning everlasting
display. Wrap the pot in a co-ordinating fabric to finish off the arrangement.*

MATERIALS
_____

*small flowerpot
square of fabric to cover the pot
knife
small florist's dry foam cone
4 florist's stub wires
florist's dry foam cone,
about 18 cm / 7 in tall
scissors
bunch of dried blue larkspur
florist's wire, if necessary
bunch of dried
yellow strawflowers*

1

Stand the pot in the centre of the fabric and
tuck the corners into the pot. Tuck in any
other loose portions of fabric.

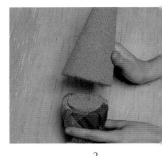

2

Cut down the small foam cone to fit
inside of the pot. Position four stub w
so they project above the foam. Use t
for attaching the top cone.

3

Snip the florets off the larkspur, leavin
small stalks to push into the foam. Mak
rows of larkspur down the length of th
to quarter it; then fill in either side of
rows to create broad blue bands. Many
florets' stalks will be strong enough to
the foam. If not, wire the florets wi
florist's wire. Finally, fill in the pan
with the strawflowers.

Leaf and Petal Decorations

Decorations are so much more appealing when made from all things natural.
These, made from preserved oak and beech leaves and dried hydrangea flowers,
are easy to do, and they make delightful tree or table decorations.

MATERIALS

scissors
dried mop-head hydrangeas
(about two for every ball)
hot glue gun and glue sticks
florist's dry foam balls, about
7.5 cm / 3 in in diameter
glycerined beech leaves
glycerined or dyed, dried
oak leaves
picture framer's wax gilt

1

Snip the florets off the mop-head hydrangeas.
Put aside the florets that have the prettiest
colouring on the top-side of the petals. Leave
a little stalk on these, but trim the stalks off
the rest. Carefully glue a floret top-side
down on to a florist's ball.

2

Continue to glue the florets face downwards
until the ball is completely covered.

3

tiny spot of glue on the back of each of
petals of a reserved floret. Fix this,
ide up, on to the ball – over the base
ng of petals. If you leave a little stalk
florets you set aside for the top layer,
n be used to help attach it to the ball.
glue work just where the petals touch
all, allowing them to curl naturally at
ges to provide texture. Continue until
all is covered. To make the leaf balls,
gild the beech leaves with wax gilt.
the beech and oak leaves over the ball,
ping them slightly to cover the foam.

Hydrangea Pot

Dried materials can be used to make the simplest, yet most exquisite, gifts.
Here's an easy but effective idea, using a single hydrangea head.

MATERIALS

glue
dyed, dried oak leaf
small flowerpot
dyed raffia
scissors
dried mop-head hydrangea

1

Use a spot of glue to attach the leaf to the pot, and then tie it on with raffia. Secure the raffia tie at the back with another spot of glue.

2

Cut the hydrangea stalk short enough s the head rests on the pot. Place the ▶ in the pot.

Spice Pots

For a cook, make a cornucopia of culinary flavourings by putting different dried
herbs and spices into terracotta pots and packing the pots in a wire basket.

MATERIALS

cinnamon sticks
dried bay leaves
garlic
dried red chillies
small flowerpots
wire basket
wire
raffia

1

Place the herbs and spices in the pots and place the pots in the basket.

2

Bend a piece of wire into a heart shap bind it with raffia. Leave a long end before starting to bind. When bindi complete, the end can be used to tie the to the basket. Finish with a bow.

Leafy Pictures

Delicate skeletonized leaves come in such breathtakingly exquisite forms that they deserve to be shown off. Mount them on hand-made papers and frame them to make simple yet stunning natural collages.

MATERIALS

*wooden picture frame
sandpaper
paint
paintbrush
backing paper
pencil
scissors
skeletonized leaf
picture framer's wax gilt
hot glue gun and glue sticks
mounting paper*

1

Take the frame apart and sand it down to provide a key before painting. A translucent colourwash has been used for painting here, but any paint will do.

2

Allow the paint to dry, then sand paint back so you're left with a woode with shading in the mouldings, p veil of colour on the surface.

3

Use the hardboard back of the frame as a template for the backing paper. Draw around it with a pencil to form a cutting line.

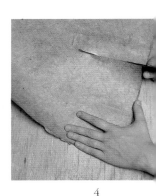

4

Cut the backing paper out.

5

are the leaf by rubbing with picture
s wax gilt. This does take a little time
the gilt has to be well worked in.

6

he backing paper on the frame back,
e mounting paper in the centre and
the leaf on to that. Here, the leaf is
with the stalk breaking the edge of
mounting paper. Finally, put the
frame back together.

Natural Christmas Decorations

Raid the pantry and scrap box, add garden clippings and dried fruit slices, and you have all the ingredients for delightful decorations that can be individually tied to a tree, or strung on to twine to make a garland. Hung from a window, the light will shine through the fruit and sparkle on the gilded twigs.

MATERIALS

florist's stub wires
twigs
picture framer's wax gilt
dried bay leaves
dried pear slices
scraps of fabric, including green
thick and thin dried apple slices
dried orange slices
small rubber bands
short lengths of cinnamon sticks
gold twine
ends of rolled beeswax candles

1

Wind florist's stub wires around the twigs to make small bundles. Rub a little gilt wax along the twigs with your finger.

2

Make up the fruit bundles. Bend a loop at one end of a florist's stub w Thread on some bay leaves, and then slice, passing the wire through the i the top and bottom. Bend a hook a top of the wire.

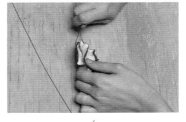

3

Tie a scrap of coloured fabric to the bottom loop and a scrap of green (synthetic chiffon is shown) at the top, to look like leaves. Make the apple-slice bundles in the same way, threading on several thicker apple slices, followed by bay leaves.

4

Wire up pairs of thinner apple slices by passing a wire through the centre and twisting the wire ends together at the top. Wire up the orange slices in the same way.

5

Use small rubber bands to make up of cinnamon sticks.

6

Either hang each decoration directly on the tree, or make up a garland to hang on the tree or at the window. Here, they have been strung together using gold twine. The beeswax candle ends are simply knotted in at intervals.

Everlasting Christmas Tree

This delightful little tree, made from dyed, preserved oak leaves and decorated with tiny gilded cones, would make an enchanting Christmas decoration. Make several and then group them to make a centrepiece, or place one at each setting.

MATERIALS

knife
bunch of dyed, dried oak leaves
florist's wire
small fir cones
picture framer's wax gilt
flowerpot, 18 cm/7 in tall
small florist's dry foam cone
4 florist's stub wires
florist's dry foam cone,
about 18 cm/7 in tall

1

Cut the leaves off the branches and trim the stalks. Wire up bunches of about four leaves, making some bunches with small leaves, some with medium-sized leaves and others with large leaves. Sort the bunches into piles.

3

Prepare the pot by cutting the smaller foam cone to fit the pot, adding stub-wire stakes and positioning the larger cone on to this. Attach the leaves to the cone, starting at the top with the bunches of small leaves, and working down through the medium and large leaves to make a realistic shape. Add the gilded cones to finish.

2

Insert wires into the bottom end of each fir cone and twist the ends together. Gild each cone by rubbing on wax gilt.

Fruity Tree

Glycerined leaves make a perfect foundation for any dried topiary. You can buy them in branches, ready glycerined for use, or glycerine your own garden prunings. Here, they have been wired into bunches for a fabulous, full look.

MATERIALS

*secateurs
3 branches of glycerined
beech leaves
florist's stub wires
dried pear slices
florist's dry foam ball, about
13 cm/5 in diameter
flowerpot, 18 cm/7 in tall*

1

e leaves off the branches and trim the
ks short. Wire up small bunches of
r six beech leaves and twist the ends
of the wires together.

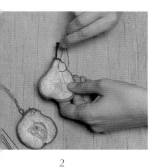

2

stub wire through the top of each pear
lice and twist the ends together.

3

Completely cover the portion of the ball that
will show above the pot with beech leaves.

4

Add the pear slices and put the ball
into the pot.

Spice Topiary

*Fashion a delightfully aromatic, culinary topiary from cloves and star anise,
put it in a terracotta pot decorated with cinnamon sticks and top with a
cinnamon-stick cross. Sticking all the cloves into the florist's foam is
both easy to do and wonderfully therapeutic.*

MATERIALS

small 'long Tom' terracotta flowerpot
knife
cinnamon sticks
hot glue gun and glue sticks
florist's foam cone for dried flowers,
about 23 cm/9 in tall
smaller florist's foam cone
florist's stub wires
large pack of star anise (containing
about 20)
cloves

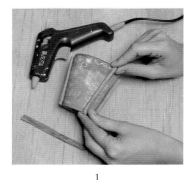

1

Prepare the pot by cutting the cinnamon
sticks to the length of the pot and gluing
them in position.

2

Trim the top of the larger cone. Cut
smaller cone to fit inside the pot. Pu
stub wires upright in the pot so they
above the foam.

3

Use these wires to stake the trimmed cone
on top of the foam-filled pot.

4

Sort out all the complete star anise fro
pack, plus any that are almost compl
you'll need about 20 in all. Wire the
by passing a wire over the front in
direction, and another wire over the
in another direction so that they cross
other. Twist the wires together at
back and trim to about 1 cm/½ i

5

the star anise into the cone in rows –
three down each side to quarter the
Put two vertically between each row.
fill the remaining area of cone with
ves, packing them tightly so none
of the foam shows through.

6

two short pieces of cinnamon stick
orm a cross. Wire this up, and use
to decorate the top of the topiary.

Dried-flower Pot

Dried flowers always look their best when the blooms are massed and the stalks not too prominent. Here's a charming treatment: roses and lavender tucked into a tiny terracotta pot, and then tied around with raffia.

MATERIALS

knife
small florist's dry foam cone
small 'long Tom' flowerpot
dried rosebuds
scissors or secateurs
dried lavender
dyed raffia
hot glue gun and glue sticks

1

Trim the foam to fit the pot. Place the rosebuds around the edge of the pot.

2

Cut the lavender stalks to about 1 cm and use them to fill the centre of arrangement. Tie a dyed raffia bow a the pot and secure it at the back w a spot of glue.

Everlasting Basket

Hydrangeas look fabulous dried, providing a flamboyant display that can simply be massed into a basket. They're also about the easiest flowers to dry at home. Just put the cut flowers in about 1 cm/½ in of water and leave them. The flowers will take up the water and then gradually dry out.

MATERIALS

knife
florist's dry foam
painted wooden basket
dried mop-head hydrangeas
dried globe artichokes
ribbon

1

...t the florist's foam to fit and fill the
...ket, and then arrange the hydrangeas
to cover the top of the basket.

2

Add the dried globe artichoke at one end
for texture.

3

Tie a ribbon to the handle of the basket
to finish.

Dried-herb Wreath

A dried-herb wreath based on lavender makes a wonderful, textural, aromatic wall hanging. This one also incorporates mugwort, tarragon, lovage and large French lavender seedheads.

MATERIALS

scissors
florist's wire
dried lavender
dried mugwort
dried lovage
dried tarragon
hot glue gun and glue sticks
small wreath base
French lavender seedheads

1

Wire all the dried herbs and flowers, except the French lavender seedheads, into small bunches.

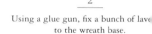

2

Using a glue gun, fix a bunch of lave to the wreath base.

3

Next, glue a bunch of mugwort to the wreath base.

4

Work round the base, adding a bunch of lovage.

5

Continue all round the wreath, intersp the different bunches of herbs to co completely, using the tarragon to ad feathery look.

6

Finally, for structure, add the indivi French lavender seedheads.

Love and Kisses Collage

This witty natural collage is made from tropical seedheads and cinnamon sticks mounted on linen muslin. Even the frame has been decorated with giant cinnamon sticks, glued over a simple wooden frame.

MATERIALS

*wooden picture frame
brown backing paper
scissors
linen muslin
hot glue gun and glue sticks
knife
small cinnamon sticks
florist's wire
heart-shaped or any other large
tropical seedheads
4 very large cinnamon sticks*

1

Take the glass out of the picture frame and stick the backing paper to the hardboard backing. Cut the linen muslin to size, and fray the edges. Put spots of glue all around the edge of the muslin and then stick it to the backing.

2

Glue six short lengths of cinnamon into three crosses, then wire them up to form a delicate metallic cross joint.

3

Glue the heart-shaped seedheads to th[e] of the picture. Glue the cinnamon 'ki[sses'] to the bottom.

4

Finish by making a cinnamon-stick frame. Cut two very large cinnamon sticks to the same length as the frame and two to the same as the width. Glue a stick to the top of the frame, then another to the bottom. Next, glue the side ones to these.

Decorative Dried Artichokes

The exquisite pinky shades at the base of some dried globe artichokes are too beautiful to be covered up by containers. Show them off by balancing the artichokes across pots covered in linen muslin to make wonderful natural decorations.

MATERIALS

small flowerpot
square of linen muslin
dyed raffia
dried globe artichokes with
a pinky purple hue

1

Place the pot in the centre of the linen muslin and tuck the fabric corners into the pot.

2

Tuck in any other loose ends, and then tie everything in place with raffia. Make an arrangement by balancing the artichokes on the pot to show off the depth of colour on the undersides.

Spicy Pomander

Pomanders were originally nature's own air fresheners. The traditional orange pomanders are fairly tricky to do, because the critical drying process can so easily go wrong, leading to mouldy oranges. This one, made of cloves and cardamom pods offers none of those problems, and makes a refreshing change in soft muted colours.

MATERIALS

cloves
florist's dry foam ball,
about 7.5 cm / 3 in diameter
hot glue gun and glue sticks
green cardamom pods
raffia
florist's stub wire

1

Start by making a single line of cloves all around the circumference of the ball. Make another one in the other direction, so you have divided the ball into quarters.

2

Make a line of cloves on both sides of original lines to make broad bands of quartering the ball.

3

Starting at the top of the first quarter, glue cardamom pods over the foam, methodically working in rows to create a neat effect. Repeat on the other three quarters.

4

Tie a bow in the centre of a length of Pass a stub wire through the knot a twist the ends together.

5

Fix the bow to the top of the ball
using the stub wire.

6

Join the two loose ends in a knot
for hanging the pomander.

Country Gifts

*What can bring more pleasure than gifts inspired
by country traditions? They have a quality that
acknowledges the seasons and withstands the test
of time. Gather together all the natural materials
you can find — shells, papers, natural fabrics,
wire, and even chicken wire — and turn them
into something very special.*

Sleep Pillow

Many people still swear by sleep pillows, which are traditionally filled with chamomile and hops. Since hops are related to the cannabis plant, they induce a feeling of sleepy well-being, while chamomile helps you to relax. Either buy ready-prepared sleep mix, or make up your own with chamomile, lemon verbena and a few hops. Stitch a pillow filled with these relaxing herbs to keep on your bed, and look forward to some good night's sleep.

MATERIALS

*linen muslin, 2m × 20 cm/
80 × 8 in (this can be made up
of two or more shorter lengths)
pins, needle and thread
scissors
pure cotton fabric, 50 × 25 cm/
20 × 10 in
herbal sleep mix
1 m/39 in antique lace
1 m/39in ribbon,
1 cm/½ in wide
4 pearl buttons*

1

Prepare the linen muslin border by stitching together enough lengths to make up 2m/80 in. With right sides facing, stitch the ends together to form a ring. Trim the seam. Fold the ring in half lengthways with wrong sides facing and run a line of gathering stitches close to the raw edges.

2

Cut two pieces of cotton fabric into 25 × 10 in squares. Pull up the gathering th of the muslin to fit the cushion edge. P to the right side of one square, with r edges facing outwards, matching the edges and easing the gathers evenly ro the cushion. Put the second square on and pin the corners. Stitch the seam leaving a gap for stuffing. Trim the sea

3

Turn the cushion right-side out and fi with herbal sleep mix. Stitch the gap enclose the border.

4

...ing tiny stitches, sew the lace to the
...cushion about 2.5 cm / 1 in away
from the border.

5

...the ribbon close to the lace, making a
...neat diagonal fold at the corners.

6

...nish by sewing a tiny pearl button
to each corner.

Herb Pot-mat

Protect tabletops from hot pots and pans with an aromatic mat, filled with cinnamon, cloves and bay leaves. The heat of the pot immediately releases the piquancy of its contents, kept evenly distributed with mattress-style ties.

MATERIALS

scissors
ticking, at least 62 × 55 cm /
25 × 22 in
pins, needle and thread

spice mix to fill, e.g. dried bay
leaves, cloves, cinnamon sticks
heavy-duty upholstery needle
cotton string

1

First make the hanger by cutting a strip of ticking 5 × 30cm / 2 × 12in. With right sides facing, fold this in half lengthways. Stitch the long side, leaving the ends open. Trim the seam. Turn right side out and press. Fold in half to form a loop. Cut two rectangles from the fabric measuring about 62 × 50cm / 25 × 20in.

2

Place the cushion pieces on a flat surface, right sides facing, and then slip the hanging loop between the layers, with the raw edges pointing out towards a corner.

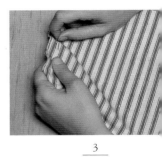

3

Pin and stitch the cushion pieces toge[ther] leaving about 7.5cm / 3 in open. Trim seams. Turn right side out.

4

Fill the cushion with the spices.

5

Slip-stitch to close the opening.

6

Using a heavy-duty upholstery nee[dle] threaded with cotton string, make a st[itch] about a third in from two sides of t[he] cushion, clearing the spices inside the[m] away from the area as you go. Untwis[t] strands of the string for a more feathery [effect]. Repeat with three other ties to give mattress effect. Make a simple kno[t] in each to secure the ties.

Lavender Sachets

Use fabric scraps to appliqué simple motifs on to charming chequered fabrics, and then stitch them into sachets to fill with lavender and use as drawer-fresheners. Inspired by traditional folk art, these have universal appeal.

MATERIALS

scissors
fabric scraps
paper for templates
pins, needle and thread
stranded embroidery thread in
different colours
loose dried lavender
button

1

Cut two pieces of fabric into squares a 15 cm/6in. If you are using a checke striped fabric, it is a good idea to let design dictate the exact size. Scale up template and use it as a pattern to cu and wing shapes from contrasting fat Pin and tack the bird shape to th right side of one square.

2

Neatly slip-stitch the bird shape to the sachet front, turning in the edges as you go. Repeat with the wing shape.

3

Using three strands of embroidery thread in a contrasting colour, make neat running stitches around the bird and its wing.

4

Make long stitches on the tail and wi indicate feathers, graduating them ir pleasing shape. Sew in the button e

5

With right sides facing, stitch the fro back of the sachet together, leaving 5 cm/2 in gap. Trim the seams. Tu right-side out and press. Fill with d lavender, and then slip-stitch to close th

Lacy Lavender Heart

Evocative of the Victorian era, this exquisitely pretty heart-shaped lavender bag is made from simple, creamy muslin, and trimmed with antique lace and satin ribbon. The chiffon ribbon at the top is tied into a loop for hanging on coat hangers with favourite garments.

MATERIALS

paper for template
scissors
silky muslin, about
60 × 20 cm/24 × 8in

pins, needle and stranded
embroidery thread
pearl button
loose dried lavender

50 cm/20in antique lace
50 cm/20 in very narrow
satin ribbon
50 cm/20 in medium ribbon

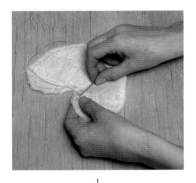

1

Make a heart-shaped paper template about 15 cm/6 in high and use this as a pattern. Cut four heart shapes from muslin. Tack the hearts together in pairs so each heart is a double thickness of muslin.

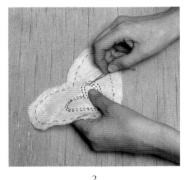

2

Cut a smaller heart shape from muslin. Carefully stitch this to the centre front of one of the larger heart shapes, using two strands of embroidery thread and a running stitch. Make another row of running stitches inside this.

3

Sew the button to the top of the smaller heart.

4

Stitch a third row of running stitches the other two. Allow the edges of the s heart to fray. With right sides facing, all around the edge of the two large d thickness muslin heart shapes, leaving of 5 cm/2 in. Trim the seams, snip the seam at the 'V' of the heart and sn the bottom point within the seam allo Turn the heart right-side out. Fill w lavender and slip-stitch to close the Don't despair if the heart looks pre miserable and misshapen at this sta

5

lly slip-stitch the lace around the edge
of the heart.

6

n the satin ribbon over the lower edge
of the lace.

7

with a ribbon bow, arranging it so the
tails are upwards as these can then be
ned to form a loop for hanging on
coat hangers in the wardrobe.

Herb Bath-bag

*Enjoy a traditional herbal bath by filling a fine muslin bag with relaxing herbs,
tying it to the taps and letting the hot water run through. This draw-string
design means it can be re-used time after time, if you keep refilling it with new
herbs. Chamomile and hops are relaxing; basil and sage are invigorating.*

MATERIALS

*silky muslin, about 30 × 40 cm /
12 × 16 in
pins, needle and thread*

*scissors
fabric scraps, for casing
1 m / 39 in narrow ribbon*

*safety pin
herb bath-mix or any combination
of dried herbs*

1

With right sides facing, fold over about
5cm / 2in of the silky muslin at both short
ends, pin and stitch each side. Trim the
seams. Turn right-side out.

2

Turn in and hem the raw edges of the
folded-over ends.

3

Cut two strips of cotton fabric abo
2.5 cm / 1 in wide and as long as the
of the muslin, with about 5 mm / ¼in
for turnings all round. Iron a hem a
both long edges. Turn in and hem the
then pin one casing on the right side
muslin so the bottom edge of the casin
up with the hem line. Neatly stitch
casing in place along both long sea
Repeat with the other casing.

4

With right sides together, fold the mu
half so the casings line up. Stitch the
seams from the bottom edge of the ca
the bottom edge of the bag. Trim the

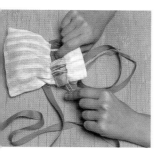

5

...he ribbon in half, attach a safety pin to
... end and use this to thread the ribbon
...gh the casing so both ends finish up at
... same side. Remove the safety pin.

6

...n the safety pin to one end of the other
... of ribbon and thread it through the
...g in the other direction so the ends
...nish up at the other side. Fill with
herbs ready for use.

Shell Pot

Decorate a flowerpot with shells and some old netting, and then use it to hold plants, pencils, paintbrushes, strings, ribbon, or any paraphernalia that needs to be kept in check. It's a pretty and inexpensive way to make a very special container.

MATERIALS

*small net bag
flowerpot, 18 cm / 7 in tall
scissors
hot glue gun and glue sticks
thick string
small cowrie shells
cockle shells
starfish or similar central motif*

1

Slip the net bag over the flowerpot and trim the top edge. Secure it by gluing on a length of string.

2

Using a glue gun, position a row of c shells along the top edge.

3

Glue cockle shells around the rim; po the starfish and four cockle shells at the

Shell Box

A simple brown-paper box takes on a South-Seas feel when decorated with half-cowries. Available from craft shops, their flattened bottoms make them easy to stick to surfaces. Here, some have also been strung together to make a toggle for fastening.

MATERIALS

hot glue gun and glue sticks
raffia
small buff box
half-courie shells
upholstery needle

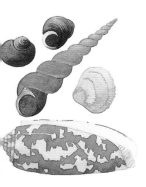

1

a loop of raffia from the bottom of the
ox, up the back and along the top.

2

Tie half-cowries into a bunch on a length of
raffia, tying each one in separately. Leave a
short length of raffia free. Pierce the front of
the box with an upholstery needle and thread
the raffia through. Knot it on the inside.

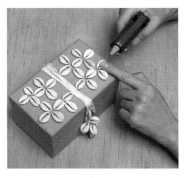

3

Glue on a pattern of half-cowries to decorate
the outside of the box.

Shell Candle Centrepiece

An old flowerpot, scallop shells gleaned from the fishmonger or kitchen and smaller shells picked up from the beach make up a fabulous, Venus-inspired table-centrepiece. Either put a candle in the centre, as here, or fill it with dried fruits or flowers.

MATERIALS

hot glue gun and glue sticks
8 curved scallop shells
flowerpot, 18 cm / 7 in tall
bag of cockle shells
4 flat scallop shells
newspaper, florist's foam or
other packing material
saucer
candle
raffia

1

Generously apply hot glue to the ins lower edge of a large curved scallop s Hold it in place on the rim of the pot few seconds until it is firmly stuck. Co sticking shells to the top of the po arranging them so they overlap sligh until the whole of the rim has been co

2

In the same way, glue a cockle shell where two scallops join. Continue all around the pot.

3

Place another row of cockles at the joins of the first row. Glue flat scallop shells face upwards to the bottom of the pot, first at the front, then at the back, and then the two sides, to ensure the pot stands straight.

4

Fill the pot with packing material and a saucer on top of this. Stand a cand on the saucer.

5

Tie raffia around the pot where it joins the stand.

6

Decorate the stand with a few more cockles, if you like. Stand a few more curved scallop shells inside the original row to create a fuller, more petalled shape.

Shell Mirror

The subtle rose-pinks of ordinary scallop shells, picked up from the fishmonger, make for an easy, eye-catching mirror surround that's also environmentally friendly. Here, four large ones have been used at the corners with smaller ones filling in the sides.

MATERIALS

sandpaper
mirror in wooden frame
paint
paintbrush
4 large flat scallop shells
hot glue gun and glue sticks
10 small flat scallop shells
seagrass string
2 metal eyelets

1

Sand down and paint the mirror frame with the colour of your choice.

3

In the same way, glue three of the smaller scallop shells to each side of the mirror.

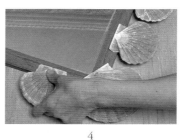

4

Attach two of the smaller scallop shells to the top of the mirror and two to the bottom.

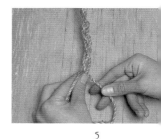

5

Plait three lengths of seagrass strin to make a hanger.

2

Position the large scallop shells at the of the mirror, using the hot glue

6

Screw metal eyelets into each side of frame at the back, and tie the hang on to these.

Chicken-wire Heart

The garden shed provided the materials for this heart. Two shapes are simply cut from chicken wire and joined to give a more three-dimensional effect; then they are decorated with string. The heart is lovely hung on the wall inside; if it is decorated with a heavy-duty garden string it could also be hung outside.

MATERIALS

newspaper, for template
scissors
chicken wire
wire cutters or secateurs
paper string or any strong string

1

Cut a heart template about 35 cm/14 in long from newspaper. Use this as a pattern to cut two heart shapes from chicken wire.

2

Place one chicken-wire heart on top of other, and bend in the edges sharply around to join the shapes.

3

Thread strong string all around the e to finish, leaving two long ends free a centre. Thread a separate piece of stri the centre top, and tie the ends togeth make a hanging loop.

COUNTRY GIFTS

....

Raffia Heart

This charming heart starts life, somewhat inauspiciously, as a coat hanger. With the hook cut off, the hanger is simply bent to shape, ready to be wrapped with raffia. A similar tiny heart, made from heavy-gauge reel wire, is hung in the centre to finish it off.

MATERIALS
_____

wire coat hanger
wire cutters or secateurs
raffia
heavy-gauge wire

1
___

d the coat hanger into a heart shape
and cut off the hook.

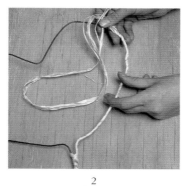

2
___

Starting at the base of the heart and leaving
a free length of raffia, wind raffia around
the heart to meet in the middle again.
Tie the two ends together.

3
___

Make a smaller heart from wire and bind it
with raffia. Use raffia to tie the smaller
heart so that it hangs inside the larger one.
Tie a hanging loop on to the larger heart.

Natural Stationery

*Add your own personal style to a simple brown-paper stationery folder
or notebook, by making closures from anything to hand.
Here, an auger shell and a bundle of cinnamon sticks make
elegant toggles, with loops made from twine and raffia.*

MATERIALS

*plain buff stationery folder
or notebook
auger shell or cinnamon stick
upholstery needle
raffia or twine
hot glue gun and glue sticks
2 small squares of brown paper*

1

Work out the best position on the stationery
folder or notebook for the shell or cinnamon
stick toggle. Using an upholstery needle,
pierce a hole in this position. Pass a loop of
raffia through this to the front. Pass a short
piece of raffia through this loop.

2

Tie the short piece of raffia around
shell or cinnamon stick. Secure
with a spot of glue.

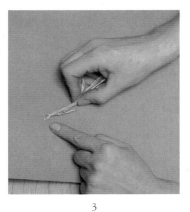

3

Open the folder or notebook. Tie a knot
in the raffia close to the cover. Trim the
ends of the raffia.

4

On the back cover, make a hole in a similar
position to the one on the front cover.
Thread a loop of raffia through this. Test the
length by bringing it around to the front
and experimenting with 'buttoning' and
'unbuttoning' the shell or stick, bearing in
mind that you will need extra slack to allow
for knotting the loop in place. Make a knot
in the raffia on the inside.

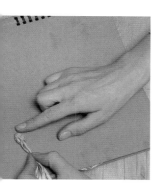

5

the folder or book and make another
close to the cover on the outside so the
is fixed firmly. Test the loop for size
, and if necessary undo the knots and
re-knot them in the right place.

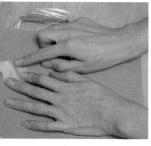

6

the knots on the insides of the covers
luing on the small squares of brown
er to avoid damage to the adjoining
s. This is also useful if you are using
terial for the loop that could stain
he pages, such as coloured twine
or a leather thong.

163

Filigree Leaf Wrap

Even the most basic brown parcel-paper can take on a very special look. Use a gilded skeletonized leaf and gold twine in combination with brown paper: chunky coir string would give a more robust look.

MATERIALS

*picture framer's wax gilt
large skeletonized leaf
brown paper
sticky tape
gold twine
hot glue gun and glue sticks,
if necessary*

1

Rub wax gilt into the skeletonized leaf.

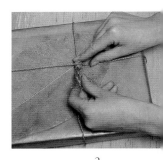

2

Wrap the parcel in the brown paper an
gilt wax on to the corners. Tie the pa
with gold twine, bringing the two e
together and tying a knot. Fray the en
create a tassle effect. Slip the leaf unde
twine, securing it with glue at each
if necessary.

Fruit and Foliage Gift-wraps

*Here, gilded brown parcel-paper provides a fitting background
for a decoration of leaves and dried fruit slices.*

MATERIALS

*brown paper
sticky tape
picture framer's wax gilt
seagrass string
hot glue gun and glue sticks
dried fruit slices
preserved leaves*

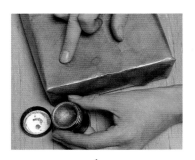

1

Wrap the parcel with brown paper and rub
in gilt wax, paying special attention
to the corners.

2

Tie the parcel with seagrass string
and then glue a different dried fru
or leaf to each quarter.

Tissue Rosette Gift-wrap

Tissue papers make a fabulous foundation for any gift-wrapping; they come in a glorious array of colours, and they softly take to any shape.

MATERIALS

*tissue paper in 2 shades
co-ordinating twine*

1

Place a cylindrical gift in the centre of two squares of tissue, one laid on top of the other. Gather the tissue up and tie it with twine.

2

Gently open out the rosette at the t

Lavender Tissue Gift-wrap

Bunches of lavender add a real country touch to tissue gift-wrap, and become part of the gift.

MATERIALS

*dried lavender
twine
tissue paper in 2 shades
sticky tape
glue*

1

Make two bunches of lavender and tie them with twine to form a cross.

2

Wrap the parcel in the darker toned paper, and then wrap it with the paler cut to form an envelope. Glue the lav to the front of the parcel.

Bath-time Bottle

Recycle a glass bottle containing home-made lotion and decorate it with corrugated card in gem-like colours for a real impact.

MATERIALS

scissors
coloured corrugated card
flower-water bottle
hot glue gun and glue sticks
coloured raffia

1	2
Cut the corrugated card to size, then glue in position around the bottle. Tie with raffia.	Make a matching label from corrugated and tie it on using raffia.

Bath-time Treat Jar

Decorate a jar of lotion to complement the bottle, using brilliantly coloured fine corrugated card. Royal blue and emerald green make a rich combination that could be used for both men and women.

MATERIALS

scissors
coloured corrugated card
baby-food jar
hot glue gun and glue sticks
twine

1	2
Cut the corrugated card to size, and then glue in place around the jar. Tie the twine around the jar.	Cut a piece of corrugated card to fit th of the lid and glue it in place. Glue tw cover the side of the lid.

COUNTRY
Cooking

LIZ TRIGG

Spring Recipes

Spring brings the first of the year's tender young vegetables, and there are plenty of tempting recipes to make the most of seasonal produce. Treat yourself to a zesty lemon cake or an Easter plait studded with fruit and spices, for an Easter tea.

Spring Roasted Chicken with Fresh Herbs and Garli

A smaller chicken or four poussins can also be roasted in this way.

INGREDIENTS

1.75 kg / 4½ lb free-range chicken
or 4 small poussins
finely grated rind and
juice of 1 lemon
1 garlic clove, crushed
30 ml / 2 tbsp olive oil
2 fresh thyme sprigs
2 fresh sage sprigs
75 g / 3 oz / 6 tbsp unsalted butter,
softened
salt and freshly ground
black pepper

Serves 4

1

Season the chicken or poussins well.
Mix the lemon rind and juice, garlic and
olive oil together and pour them over the
chicken. Leave to marinate for at least
2 hours in a non-metallic dish.
When the chicken has marinated preheat
the oven to 230°C / 450°F / Gas Mark 8.

2

Place the herbs in the cavity of the bir
smear the butter over the skin. Season
Roast the chicken for 10 minutes, ther
the oven down to 190°C / 375°F / Gas Ma
Baste the chicken well, and then roast
further 1 hour 30 minutes, until the juic
clear when the thigh is pierced with a s
Leave to rest for 15 minutes before car

Lemon and Rosemary Lamb Chops

*Spring lamb is delicious with the fresh flavour of lemon. Garnish with sprigs of
fresh rosemary – the aroma is irresistible.*

INGREDIENTS

12 lamb cutlets
45 ml / 3 tbsp olive oil
2 large rosemary sprigs
juice of 1 lemon
3 garlic cloves, sliced
salt and freshly ground
black pepper

Serves 4

1

Trim the excess fat from the cutlets.
Mix the oil, rosemary, lemon juice and
garlic together and season well.

2

Pour over the chops in a shallow dish
marinate for 30 minutes. Remove from
marinade, and blot the excess with kit
paper and grill for 10 minutes on each

Carrot and Coriander Soufflés

Use tender young carrots for this light-as-air dish.

450 g / 1 lb carrots
30 ml / 2 tbsp fresh chopped
coriander
4 eggs, separated
salt and freshly ground
black pepper

Serves 4

1

Peel the carrots.

2

Cook in boiling salted water for 20 min
or until tender. Drain, and process un
smooth in a food processor.

3

Preheat the oven to 200°C / 400°F /
Gas Mark 6. Season the puréed carrots well,
and stir in the chopped coriander.

4

Fold the egg yolks into the carrot mixt

5

In a separate bowl, whisk the egg whites
until stiff.

6

Fold the egg whites into the carrot mix
and pour into four greased ramekins. B
for about 20 minutes or until risen ar
golden. Serve immediately.

Leeks with Ham and Cheese Sauce

A tasty teatime or supper dish: use a strong cheese for best results.

INGREDIENTS

4 leeks
4 slices ham

For the sauce
25 g / 1 oz / 2 tbsp unsalted butter
25 g / 1 oz / 1 tbsp plain flour
300 ml / ½ pint / 1¼ cups milk
½ tsp French mustard
115 g / 4 oz hard cheese, grated
salt and freshly ground
black pepper

Serves 4

1

Preheat the oven to 190°C / 375°F /
Gas Mark 5. Trim the leeks to 2 cm / 1 in of
the white and cook in salted water for about
20 minutes until soft. Drain thoroughly.
Wrap the leeks in the ham slices.

2

To make the sauce, melt the butter in
saucepan. Add the flour and cook for a
minutes. Remove from the heat and
gradually add the milk, whisking well w
each addition. Return to the heat and wl
until the sauce thickens. Stir in the mus
and 75 g / 3 oz of the cheese and season v
Lay the leeks in a shallow ovenproof dish
pour over the sauce. Scatter the extra ch
on top and bake for 20 minutes.

Baked Eggs with Double Cream and Chives

This is a rich dish best served with Melba toast: it's very easy and quick to make.

INGREDIENTS

15 g / ½ oz / 1 tbsp unsalted
butter, softened
60 ml / 4 tbsp double cream
15 ml / 1 tbsp snipped fresh chives
4 eggs
50 g / 2 oz Gruyère cheese,
finely grated
salt and freshly ground
black pepper

Serves 2

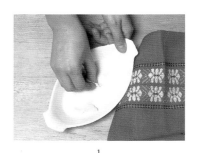

1

Preheat the oven to 180°C / 350°F /
Gas Mark 4. Grease two individual gratin
dishes. Mix the cream with the chives,
and season with salt and pepper.

2

Break the eggs into each dish and top w
the cream mixture. Sprinkle the chees
around the edges of the dishes and bake
the oven for 15–20 minutes. When cool
brown the tops under the grill for a mir

Lemon Drizzle Cake

You can also make this recipe using a large orange instead of the lemons;
either way, it makes a zesty treat for afternoon tea.

INGREDIENTS

finely grated rind of 2 lemons
175 g / 6 oz / 12 tbsp caster sugar
225 g / 8 oz / 1 cup unsalted
butter, softened
4 eggs
225 g / 8 oz / 2 cups self-raising
flour
5 ml / 1 tsp baking powder
¼ tsp salt
shredded rind of 1 lemon,
to decorate

For the syrup
juice of 1 lemon
150 g / 5 oz / ¾ cup caster sugar

Serves 6

1

Preheat the oven to 160°C/325°F/
Gas Mark 3. Grease a 1 kg/2 lb loaf tin or
18–20 cm/7–8 in round cake tin and line it
with greaseproof paper or baking parchment.
Mix the lemon rind and caster sugar together.

2

Cream the butter with the lemon and s
mixture. Add the eggs and mix unt
smooth. Sift the flour, baking powder
salt into a bowl and fold a third at a time
the mixture. Turn the batter into the
smooth the top and bake for 1½ hours
until golden brown and springy to the t

3

To make the syrup, slowly heat the ju
with the sugar and dissolve it gently. M
several slashes in the top of the cake and
over the syrup. Sprinkle the shredded le
rind and 5 ml/1 tsp granulated sugar o
and leave to cool.

Wholemeal Bread

Home-made bread creates one of the most evocative smells in country cooking.
Eat this on the day of making, to enjoy the superb fresh taste.

INGREDIENTS

20 g / ¾ oz fresh yeast
300 ml / ½ pint / 1 ¼ cups
lukewarm milk
5 ml / 1 tsp caster sugar
225 g / 8 oz / 1 ½ cups strong
wholemeal flour, sifted
225 g / 8 oz / 2 cups strong
white flour, sifted
5 ml / 1 tsp salt
50 g / 2 oz / 4 tbsp butter,
chilled and cubed
1 egg, lightly beaten
30 ml / 2 tbsp mixed seeds

Makes 4 rounds or 2 loaves

1

Gently dissolve the yeast with a little of the
milk and the sugar to make a paste. Place
both the flours plus any bran from the sieve
and the salt in a large warmed mixing bowl.
Rub in the butter until the mixture
resembles breadcrumbs.

2

Add the yeast mixture, remaining milk and
egg and mix into a fairly soft dough. Knead
on a floured board for 15 minutes. Lightly
grease the mixing bowl and put the dough
back in the bowl, covering it with a piece of
greased cling film. Leave to double in size
in a warm place (this should take
at least an hour).

3

Knock the dough back and knead it for a
further 10 minutes. Preheat the oven to
200°C / 400°F / Gas Mark 6. To make round
loaves, divide the dough into four pieces and
shape them into flattish rounds. Place them
on a floured baking sheet and leave to rise
for a further 15 minutes. Sprinkle the loaves
with the mixed seeds. Bake for about
20 minutes until golden and firm.

NOTE

For tin-shaped loaves, put the knocked-back
dough into two greased loaf tins instead.
Leave to rise for a further 45 minutes and
then bake for about 45 minutes, until
the loaf sounds hollow when turned out
of the tin and knocked on the base.

Easter Plait

Serve this delicious plait sliced with butter and jam.
It is also very good toasted on the day after you made it.

INGREDIENTS

200 ml/7 fl oz/⅞ cup milk
2 eggs, lightly beaten
450 g/1 lb/4 cups plain flour
½ tsp salt
10 ml/2 tsp ground mixed spice
75 g/3 oz/6 tbsp butter
20 g/¾ oz dried yeast
75 g/3 oz/6 tbsp caster sugar

175 g/6 oz/1¼ cups currants
25 g/1 oz/¼ cup candied mixed
peel, chopped
a little sweetened milk, to glaze
25 g/1 oz/1½ tbsp glacé
cherries, chopped
15 g/½ oz/1 tbsp angelica,
chopped

Serves 8

1

Warm the milk to lukewarm, add two-thirds of it to the eggs and mix well.

2

Sift the flour, salt and mixed spice together. Rub in the butter, then add the sugar and dried yeast. Make a well in the centre, and add the milk mixture, adding more milk as necessary to make a sticky dough.

3

Knead on a well-floured surface and t
knead in the currants and mixed pe
reserving 15 ml/1 tbsp for the topping
the dough in a lightly greased bowl a
cover it with a damp tea towel. Leave
double its size. Preheat the oven to
220°C/425°F/Gas Mark 7.

4

Turn the dough out on to a floured surface and knead again for 2–3 minutes. Divide the dough into three even pieces. Roll each piece into a sausage shape roughly 20cm/8 in long. Plait the three pieces together, turning under and pinching each end. Place on a floured baking sheet and leave to rise for 15 minutes.

5

Brush the top with sweetened milk a
scatter with roughly chopped cherries,
of angelica and the reserved mixed pe
Bake in the preheated oven for 45 minu
until the bread sounds hollow when ta
on the bottom. Cool slightly on a wire

Orange-blossom Jelly

A fresh orange jelly makes a delightful dessert: the natural fruit flavour combined with the smooth jelly has a cleansing quality that is especially welcome after a rich main course. This is delicious served with thin, crisp langues de chat *biscuits.*

INGREDIENTS

65 g / 2½ oz / 5 tbsp caster sugar
150 ml / ¼ pint / ⅔ cup water
2 sachets of gelatine
(about 25 g / 1 oz)
600 ml / 1 pint / 2½ cups freshly
squeezed orange juice
30 ml / 2 tbsp orange-flower water

Serves 4–6

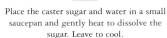

1

Place the caster sugar and water in a small saucepan and gently heat to dissolve the sugar. Leave to cool.

2

Sprinkle over the gelatine, ensuring it is completely submerged in the water. Leave stand until the gelatine has absorbed all liquid and is solid.

3

Gently melt the gelatine over a bowl of simmering water until it becomes clear and transparent. Leave to cool. When the gelatine is cold, mix it with the orange juice and orange-flower water.

4

Wet a jelly mould and pour in the jelly. Chill in the refrigerator for at least 2 hours or until set. Turn out to serve.

Rhubarb and Orange Crumble

The almonds give this crumble topping a nutty taste and crunchy texture.
This crumble is extra-delicious with home-made custard.

INGREDIENTS

900 g/2 lb rhubarb, cut in
5 cm/2 in lengths
75 g/3 oz/6 tbsp caster sugar
finely grated rind and juice
of 2 oranges

115 g/4 oz/1 cup plain flour
115 g/4 oz/ ½ cup unsalted
butter, chilled and cubed
75 g/3 oz/6 tbsp demerara sugar
115 g/4 oz/1¼ cups ground almonds

Serves 6

1

Preheat the oven to 180°C/350°F/
Gas Mark 4. Place the rhubarb in a shallow
ovenproof dish.

2

Sprinkle over the caster sugar and add the
orange rind and juice.

3

Sift the flour into a mixing bowl and a[dd]
butter. Rub the butter into the flour [until]
the mixture resembles breadcrumb[s]

4

Add the demerara sugar and ground
almonds and mix well.

5

Spoon the crumble mixture over the fr[uit]
cover it completely. Bake for 40 min[utes]
until the top is browned and the fru[it is]
cooked. Serve warm.

Summer Recipes

*The warm, lazy days and long nights of summer
provide the perfect excuse for outdoor dining
with friends and family. Try Mediterranean quiche
or a glorious garden salad with nasturtium flowers.
Cooling treats include strawberry fool, or
home-made mint ice cream.*

Mackerel with Roasted Blueberries

Fresh blueberries burst with flavour when roasted, and their sharpness complements the rich flesh of mackerel very well.

INGREDIENTS

15 g / ½ oz / 2 tsp plain flour
4 small cooked, smoked mackerel fillets
50 g / 2 oz / 4 tbsp unsalted butter
juice of ½ lemon
salt and freshly ground black pepper

For the roasted blueberries
450 g / 1 lb blueberries
25 g / 1 oz / 2 tbsp caster sugar
15 g / ½ oz / 1 tbsp unsalted butter
salt and freshly ground black pepper

Serves 4

1

Preheat the oven to 200°C/400°F/ Gas Mark 6. Season the flour. Dip each fish fillet into the flour to coat it well.

2

Dot the butter on the fillets and bake i oven for 20 minutes.

3

Place the blueberries, sugar, butter a seasoning in a separate small roasting and roast them, basting them occasion for 15 minutes. To serve, drizzle th lemon juice over the roasted macker accompanied by the roasted blueberri

Griddled Trout with Bacon

This dish can also be cooked on the barbecue.

INGREDIENTS

25 g / 1 oz / 1 tbsp plain flour
4 trout, cleaned and gutted
75 g / 3 oz streaky bacon
50 g / 2 oz / 4 tbsp butter
15 ml / 1 tbsp olive oil
juice of ½ lemon
salt and freshly ground
black pepper

Serves 4

1

Pat the trout dry with kitchen roll and
mix the flour and seasoning together.

2

Roll the trout in the seasoned flour mixture
and wrap tightly in the streaky bacon.
Heat a heavy frying pan. Heat the butter and
oil in the pan and fry the trout for 5 minutes
on each side. Serve immediately, with the
lemon juice drizzled on top.

Mediterranean Quiche

*The strong Mediterranean flavours of tomatoes, peppers and anchovies
complement beautifully the cheesy pastry in this unusual quiche.*

INGREDIENTS

For the pastry
225 g / 8 oz / 2 cups plain flour
pinch of salt
pinch of dry mustard
115 g / 4 oz / ½ cup butter,
chilled and cubed
50 g / 2 oz Gruyère cheese, grated

For the filling
50 g / 2 oz can of anchovies in oil,
drained
50 ml / 2 floz / ¼ cup milk
30 ml / 2 tbsp French mustard
45 ml / 3 tbsp olive oil
2 large Spanish onions, sliced
1 red pepper, seeded and
very finely sliced
3 egg yolks
350 ml / 12 floz / 1½ cups
double cream
1 garlic clove, crushed
175 g / 6 oz mature Cheddar
cheese, grated
2 large tomatoes, thickly sliced
salt and freshly ground
black pepper
30 ml / 2 tbsp chopped fresh basil,
to garnish

Serves 8

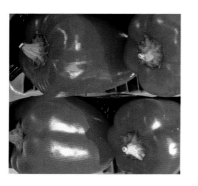

1

First make the pastry. Place the flour, salt
and mustard powder in a food processor,
add the butter and process the mixture
until it resembles breadcrumbs.

2

Add the cheese and process again brie
Add enough iced water to make a stiff do
it will be ready when the dough forms a
Wrap with cling film and chill for 30 mi

3

Meanwhile, make the filling. Soak the
anchovies in the milk for 20 minutes.
Drain away the milk.

4

Roll out the chilled pastry and line a 23
9 in loose-based flan tin. Spread over
mustard and chill for a further 15 min

5

Preheat the oven to 200°C / 400°F /
Gas Mark 6. Heat the oil in a frying pa
cook the onions and red pepper until s
In a separate bowl, beat the egg yolk
cream, garlic and Cheddar cheese toget
season well. Arrange the tomatoes in
single layer in the pastry case. Top wit
onion and pepper mixture and the anch
fillets. Pour over the egg mixture.
Bake for 30–35 minutes. Sprinkle ov
the basil and serve.

New Potato Salad

*Potatoes freshly dug up from the garden are the best. Always leave the skins on:
just wash the dirt away thoroughly. If you add the mayonnaise and other
ingredients when the potatoes are hot, the flavours will develop as the potatoes cool.*

INGREDIENTS

900 g / 2 lb baby new potatoes
2 green apples, cored and chopped
4 spring onions, chopped
3 celery sticks, finely chopped
150 ml / ¼ pint / ⅔ cup
mayonnaise
salt and freshly ground
black pepper

Serves 6

1

Cook the potatoes in salted, boiling water
for about 20 minutes, or until they are
very tender.

2

Drain the potatoes well and immediatel[y]
the remaining ingredients and stir unti[l]
mixed. Leave to cool and serve cold[.]

French Bean Salad

The secret of this recipe is to dress the beans while still hot.

INGREDIENTS

175 g / 6 oz cherry tomatoes,
halved
5 ml / 1 tsp sugar
450 g / 1 lb French beans,
topped and tailed
175 g / 6 oz feta cheese, cubed
salt and freshly ground
black pepper

For the dressing
90 ml / 6 tbsp olive oil
45 ml / 3 tbsp white-wine vinegar
¼ tsp Dijon mustard
2 garlic cloves, crushed
salt and freshly ground
black pepper

Serves 6

1

Preheat the oven to 230°C/450°F/
Gas Mark 8. Put the cherry tomatoes on a
baking sheet and sprinkle over the sugar,
salt and pepper. Roast for 10 minutes,
then leave to cool. Meanwhile, cook the
beans in boiling, salted water for 10 minutes.

2

Make the dressing by whisking togethe[r]
oil, vinegar, mustard, garlic and season[ing]
Drain the beans and immediately pour [over]
the vinaigrette and mix well. When c[ool]
stir in the roasted tomatoes and th[e]
feta cheese. Serve chilled.

Squash à la Greque

A traditional French-style dish that is usually made with mushrooms.
Make sure that you cook the baby squash until they are quite tender,
so they can fully absorb the delicious flavours of the marinade.

INGREDIENTS

175 g / 6 oz patty-pan squash
250 ml / 8 floz / 1 cup white wine
juice of 2 lemons
fresh thyme sprig
bay leaf
small bunch of fresh chervil,
roughly chopped
¼ tsp coriander seeds, crushed
¼ tsp black peppercorns, crushed
75 ml / 5 tbsp olive oil

Serves 4

1

Blanch the patty-pan squash in boiling
water for 3 minutes, and then refresh them
in cold water.

Place all the remaining ingredients in a
add 150 ml / ½ pint / ¾ cup of water a
simmer for 10 minutes, covered. Add
patty-pans and cook for 10 minutes. R
with a slotted spoon when they are co
and tender to the bite.

3

Reduce the liquid by boiling hard f
10 minutes. Strain it and pour it over
squashes. Leave until cool for the flavou
be absorbed. Serve cold.

Garden Salad

You can use any fresh, edible flowers from your garden for this beautiful salad.

INGREDIENTS

1 cos lettuce
175 g / 6 oz rocket
1 small frisée lettuce
fresh chervil and tarragon sprigs
5 ml / 1 tbsp snipped fresh chives
handful of mixed edible flower
heads, such as nasturtiums
or marigolds

For the dressing
45 ml / 3 tbsp olive oil
15 ml / 1 tbsp white-wine vinegar
½ tsp French mustard
1 garlic clove, crushed
pinch of sugar

Serves 4

1

Mix the cos, rocket and frisé leaves
and herbs together

2

Make the dressing by whisking all the
ingredients together in a large bowl. Toss the
salad leaves in the bowl with the dressing,
add the flower heads and serve at once.

Country Strawberry Fool

*Make this delicious fool on the day you want to eat it, and chill it well,
for the best strawberry taste.*

INGREDIENTS

300 ml / ½ pint / 1¼ cups milk
2 egg yolks
90 g / 3½ oz / scant ½ cup
caster sugar
few drops of vanilla essence
900 g / 2 lb ripe strawberries
juice of ½ lemon
300 ml / ½ pint / 1¼ cups double
cream

To decorate
12 small strawberries
4 fresh mint sprigs

Serves 4

1

First make the custard. Whisk 30 ml / 2 tbsp
milk with the egg yolks, 15 ml / 1 tbsp caster
sugar and the vanilla essence.

2

Heat the remaining milk until it is j
below boiling point.

3

Stir the milk into the egg mixture. Rinse
the pan out and return the mixture to it.

4

Gently heat and whisk until the mixture
thickens (it should be thick enough to coat
the back of a spoon). Lay a wet piece of
greaseproof paper on top of the custard and
leave it to cool.

5

Purée the strawberries in a food process
blender with the lemon juice and th
remaining sugar.

6

Lightly whip the cream and fold in the fruit
purée and custard. Pour into glass dishes and
decorate with the whole strawberries and
sprigs of mint.

Mint Ice Cream

This ice cream is best served slightly softened, so take it out
of the freezer 20 minutes before you want to serve it. For a special occasion,
this looks spectacular served in an ice bowl.

INGREDIENTS

8 egg yolks
75 g / 3 oz / 6 tbsp caster sugar
600 ml / 1 pint / 2½ cups single
cream
1 vanilla pod
60 ml / 4 tbsp chopped fresh mint

Serves 8

1

Beat the egg yolks and sugar until they are
pale and light using a hand-held electric
beater or a balloon whisk. Transfer to a
small saucepan.

2

In a separate saucepan, bring the cream
the boil with the vanilla pod.

3

Remove the vanilla pod and pour the hot cream
on to the egg mixture, whisking briskly.

4

Continue whisking to ensure the eggs
are mixed into the cream.

5

Gently heat the mixture until the custa
thickens enough to coat the back of a
wooden spoon. Leave to cool.

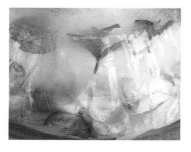

6

Stir in the mint and place in an ice-crea
maker to churn, about 3–4 hours. If yo
don't have an ice-cream maker, freeze t
ice cream until mushy and then whisk it
again, to break down the ice crystals. Fre
for another 3 hours until it is softly fro
and whisk again. Finally freeze until ha
at least 6 hours.

Mixed Berry Tart

The orange-flavoured pastry is delicious with the fresh fruits of summer.
Serve this with some extra shreds of orange rind scattered on top.

INGREDIENTS

For the pastry
225 g / 8 oz / 2 cups plain flour
115 g / 4 oz / ½ cup unsalted
butter
finely grated rind of 1 orange,
plus extra to decorate

For the filling
300 ml / ½ pint / 1¼ cups
crème fraîche
finely grated rind of 1 lemon
10 ml / 2 tsp icing sugar
675 g / 1½ lb mixed
summer berries

Serves 8

1

To make the pastry, put the flour and butter in a large bowl. Rub in the butter until the mixture resembles breadcrumbs.

2

Add the orange rind and enough cold w to make a soft dough.

3

Roll into a ball and chill for at least 30 minutes. Roll out the pastry on a lightly floured surface.

4

Line a 23 cm / 9 in loose-based flan tin v the pastry. Chill for 30 minutes. Prehea oven to 200°C / 400°F / Gas Mark 6 an place a baking sheet in the oven to heat
Line the tin with greaseproof paper ar baking beans and bake blind on the bal sheet for 15 minutes. Remove the pap and beans and bake for 10 minutes mc until the pastry is golden. Allow to cool completely. To make the filling whisk the crème fraîche, lemon rind ar sugar together and pout into the pastry Top with fruit, sprinkle with orange rind and serve sliced.

Autumn Recipes

Reap the benefits of the autumn harvest with this collection of recipes; wild mushroom tart, thyme-roasted onions and duck and chestnut casserole all make the most of autumn produce. Warming desserts such as steamed ginger and syrup pudding or poached pears, are guaranteed to keep away the autumn chill.

Wild Mushroom Tart

The flavour of wild mushrooms makes this tart really rich: use as wide a variety of mushrooms as you can get.

INGREDIENTS

For the pastry
225 g / 8 oz / 2 cups plain flour
50 g / 2 oz / 4 tbsp hard white fat
10 ml / 2 tsp lemon juice
about 150 ml / ¼ pint / ⅔ cup
ice-cold water
115 g / 4 oz / ½ cup butter,
chilled and cubed
1 egg, beaten, to glaze

For the filling
150 g / 5 oz / 10 tbsp butter
2 shallots, finely chopped
2 garlic cloves, crushed
450 g / 1 lb mixed wild
mushrooms, sliced
45 ml / 3 tbsp chopped fresh parsley
30 ml / 2 tbsp double cream
salt and freshly ground
black pepper

Serves 6

1

To make the pastry, sieve the flour and
½ tsp salt together into a large bowl.
Add the white fat and rub into the mixture
until it resembles breadcrumbs.

2

Add the lemon juice and enough iced w
to make a soft but not sticky dough
Cover and chill for 20 minutes.

3

Roll the pastry out into a rectangle on a
lightly floured surface. Mark the dough into
three equal strips and arrange half the butter
cubes over two-thirds of the dough.

4

Fold the outer two-thirds over, folding
the uncovered third last. Seal the edges
a rolling pin. Give the dough a quarter
and roll it out again. Mark it into thirds
dot with the remaining butter cube
in the same way.

5

Chill the pastry for 20 minutes. Repeat the
process of marking into thirds, folding over,
giving a quarter turn and rolling out three
times, chilling for 20 minutes in between
each time. To make the filling, melt
50 g / 2 oz / 4 tbsp butter and fry the shallots
and garlic until soft but not browned. Add
the remaining butter and the mushrooms
and cook for 35–40 minutes. Drain off any
excess liquid and stir in the remaining
ingredients. Leave to cool. Preheat the oven
to 220°C / 450°F / Gas Mark 7.

6

Divide the pastry in two. Roll out one
into a 22 cm / 9 in round, cutting aroun
plate to make a neat shape. Pile the fil
into the centre. Roll out the remainin
pastry large enough to cover the base. B
the edges of the base with water and the
the second pastry circle on top. Press
edges together to seal and brush the t
with a little beaten egg. Bake for 45 min
or until the pastry is risen, golden and f

Mushroom and Parsley Soup

*Thickened with bread, this rich mushroom soup will warm you up
on cold autumn days. It makes a terrific hearty lunch.*

INGREDIENTS

75 g / 3 oz / 6 tbsp unsalted butter
900 g / 2 lb field mushrooms,
sliced
2 onions, roughly chopped
600 ml / 1 pint / 2½ cups milk
8 slices white bread
60 ml / 4 tbsp chopped fresh parsley
300 ml / ½ pint / 1¼ cups
double cream
salt and freshly ground
black pepper

Serves 8

1

Melt the butter and sauté the mushrooms
and onions until soft but not coloured –
about 10 minutes. Add the milk.

2

Tear the bread into pieces, drop them i
the soup and leave the bread to soak f
15 minutes. Purée the soup and return
the pan. Add the parsley, cream and season
Re-heat, but do not allow the soup to b
Serve at once.

Thyme-roasted Onions

*These slowly roasted onions develop a delicious, sweet flavour which is perfect
with roast meat. You could prepare par-boiled new potatoes in the same way.*

INGREDIENTS

75 ml / 5 tbsp olive oil
50 g / 2 oz / 4 tbsp unsalted butter
900 g / 2 lb small onions
30 ml / 2 tbsp chopped fresh thyme
salt and freshly ground
black pepper

Serves 4

1

Preheat the oven to 220°C/425°F/
Gas Mark 7. Heat the oil and butter in a
large roasting tin. Add the onions and toss
them in the oil and butter mixture.

2

Add the thyme and seasoning and roast
45 minutes, basting regularly.

Duck and Chestnut Casserole

Serve this casserole with a mixture of mashed potatoes and celeriac,
to soak up the rich duck juices.

INGREDIENTS

1.75 kg / 4½ lb duck
45 ml / 3 tbsp olive oil
175 g / 6 oz small onions
50 g / 2 oz field mushrooms
50 g / 2 oz shiitake mushrooms
300 ml / ½ pint / 1¼ cups
red wine
300 ml / ½ pint / 1¼ cups
beef stock
225 g / 8 oz canned, peeled,
unsweetened chestnuts, drained
salt and freshly ground
black pepper

Serves 4–6

1

Joint the duck into eight pieces. Heat the oil
in a large frying pan and brown the duck
pieces. Remove from the frying pan.

2

Add the onions to the pan and brown th
well for 10 minutes.

3

Add the mushrooms and cook for a few
minutes more. Deglaze the pan with the
red wine and boil to reduce the volume
by half. Meanwhile, preheat the oven to
180°C / 350°F / Gas Mark 4.

4

Pour the wine and the stock into a
casserole. Replace the duck, add the
chestnuts, season well and cook in the o
for 1½ hours.

Cheese Scones

These delicious scones make a good tea-time treat. They are best served fresh and still slightly warm.

INGREDIENTS

225 g / 8 oz / 2 cups plain flour
12 ml / 2½ tsp baking powder
½ tsp dry mustard powder
½ tsp salt
50 g / 2 oz / 4 tbsp butter, chilled
75 g / 3 oz Cheddar cheese, grated
150 ml / ¼ pint / ⅔ cup milk
1 egg, beaten

Makes 12

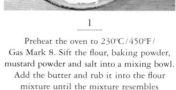

1

Preheat the oven to 230°C / 450°F / Gas Mark 8. Sift the flour, baking powder, mustard powder and salt into a mixing bowl. Add the butter and rub it into the flour mixture until the mixture resembles breadcrumbs. Stir in 50 g / 2 oz of the cheese.

2

Make a well in the centre and add the m and egg. Mix gently and then turn th dough out on to a lightly floured surfac Roll it out and cut it into traingles or squa Brush lightly with milk and sprinkle w the remaining cheese. Leave to rest fo 15 minutes, then bake them for 15 minu or until well risen.

Oatcakes

These are very simple to make and are an excellent addition to a cheese board.

INGREDIENTS

225 g / 8 oz / 1⅔ cups medium oatmeal
75 g / 3 oz / ¾ cup plain flour
1 / 4 tsp bicarbonate of soda
5 ml / 1 tsp salt
25 g / 1 oz / 2 tbsp hard white vegetable fat
25 g / 1 oz / 2 tbsp butter

Makes 24

1

Preheat the oven to 220°C / 425°F / Gas Mark 7. Place the oatmeal, flour, soda and salt in a large bowl. Gently melt the two fats together in a pan.

2

Add the melted fat and enough boiling w to make a soft dough. Turn out on to surface scattered with a little oatmeal. Roll out the dough thinly and cut it in circles. Bake the oatcakes on ungrease baking trays for 15 minutes, until crisp

Blackberry Charlotte

A classic pudding, perfect for cold days. Serve with lightly whipped cream or home-made custard.

INGREDIENTS

65 g / 2½ oz / 5 tbsp unsalted butter
175 g / 6 oz / 3 cups fresh white breadcrumbs
50 g / 2 oz / 4 tbsp soft brown sugar
60 ml / 4 tbsp golden syrup
finely grated rind and juice of 2 lemons
50 g / 2 oz walnut halves
450 g / 1 lb blackberries
450 g / 1 lb cooking apples, peeled, cored and finely sliced

Serves 4

1

Preheat the oven to 180°C / 350°F / Gas Mark 4. Grease a 450 ml / ¾ pint / 2 cup dish with 15 g / ½ oz / 1 tbsp of the butter. Melt the remaining butter and add the breadcrumbs. Sauté them for 5–7 minutes, until the crumbs are a little crisp and golden. Leave to cool slightly.

2

Place the sugar, syrup, lemon rind and j[u]ice in a small saucepan and gently warm th[rough]. Add the crumbs.

3

Process the walnuts until they are finely ground.

4

Arrange a thin layer of blackberries on the dish. Top with a thin layer of crumbs.

5

Add a thin layer of apple, topping it w[ith] another thin layer of crumbs. Repeat t[he] process with another layer of blackberr[ies] followed by a layer of crumbs. Contin[ue] until you have used up all the ingredie[nts] finishing with a layer of crumbs.

The mixture should be piled well abov[e] the top edge of the dish, because it shri[nks] during cooking. Bake for 30 minutes, u[ntil] the crumbs are golden and the fruit is s[oft].

Poached Pears

Serve warm with clotted cream and crisp shortbread fingers.

6 medium pears
350 g / 12 oz / 1¾ cups caster
sugar
75 ml / 5 tbsp runny honey
1 vanilla pod
600 ml / 1 pint / 2½ cups red wine
5 ml / 1 tsp whole cloves
7 cm / 3 in cinnamon stick

Serves 4

1

Peel the pears but leave them whole,
keeping the stalks as well.

2

Put the sugar, honey, vanilla pod, win
cloves and cinnamon stick in a large p

3

Add the pears and poach until soft, abo
30 minutes. When the pears are tende
remove them with a slotted spoon and k
them warm. Remove the vanilla pod, cl
and cinnamon stick and boil the liqui
until it is reduced by half. Serve spoon
over the pears.

Steamed Ginger and Cinnamon Syrup Pudding

A traditional and comforting steamed pudding, best served with custard.

INGREDIENTS

120 g / 4½ oz / 9 tbsp softened
butter
45 ml / 3 tbsp golden syrup
115 g / 4 oz / ½ cup caster sugar
2 eggs, lightly beaten
115 g / 4 oz / 1 cup plain flour
5 ml / 1 tsp baking powder
5 ml / 1 tsp ground cinnamon
25 g / 1 oz stem ginger,
finely chopped
30 ml / 2 tbsp milk

Serves 4

1

full steamer or saucepan of water on to
Lightly grease a 600 ml / 1 pint / 2½ cup
udding basin with 15 g / ½ oz / 1 tbsp
er. Place the golden syrup in the basin.

2

Cream the remaining butter and sugar
together until light and fluffy. Gradually
add the eggs until the mixture is glossy. Sift
the flour, baking powder and cinnamon
together and fold them into the mixture,
with the stem ginger. Add the milk to make
a soft, dropping consistency.

3

Spoon the batter into the basin and smooth
the top. Cover with a pleated piece of
greaseproof paper, to allow for expansion
during cooking. Tie securely with string and
steam for 1½–2 hours, making sure that the
water level is kept topped up, to ensure a
good flow of steam to cook the pudding.
Turn the pudding out to serve it.

French Apple Tart

For added flavour, scatter some toasted, flaked almonds over the top of this classic tart.

INGREDIENTS

For the pastry
115 g / 4 oz / ½ cup unsalted
butter, softened
50 g / 2 oz / 4 tbsp vanilla sugar
1 egg
225 g / 8 oz / 2 cups plain flour

For the filling
50 g / 2 oz / 4 tbsp unsalted butter
5 large tart apples, peeled, cored
and sliced
juice of ½ lemon
300 ml / ½ pint / 1¼ cups double
cream
2 egg yolks
25 g / 1 oz / 2 tbsp vanilla sugar
50 g / 2 oz / ⅔ cup ground
almonds, toasted
25 g / 1 oz / 2 tbsp flaked almonds,
toasted, to garnish

Serves 8

1

Place the butter and sugar in a food processor and process them well together. Add the egg and process to mix it in well.

2

Add the flour and process till you hav
soft dough. Wrap the dough in cling
and chill it for 30 minutes.

3

Roll the pastry out on a lightly floured surface to about 22–25 cm/9–10 in diameter.

4

Line a flan tin with the pastry and chi
for a further 30 minutes. Preheat the o
to 220°C/425°F/Gas Mark 7 and plac
baking sheet in the oven to heat up. Lir
pastry case with greaseproof paper an
baking beans and bake blind on the ba
sheet for 10 minutes. Then remove the
and paper and cook for a further 5 min

5

Turn the oven down to 190°C/375°F/
Gas Mark 5. To make the filling, melt the butter in a frying pan and lightly sauté the apples for 5–7 minutes. Sprinkle the apples with lemon juice.

6

Beat the cream and egg yolks with the s
Stir in the toasted ground almonds. Ar
the apple slices on top of the warm pa
and pour over the cream mixture. Bak
25 minutes, or until the cream is just s
set – it tastes better if the cream is s
slightly runny in the centre. Serve hot or
scattered with flaked almonds.

Winter Recipes

With the nights drawing in, we all need something
substantial and warming to keep out the cold.
Try roast beef with roasted peppers, or raised
country pie. Scotch pancakes or cranberry muffins
are a perfect fire-side treat, and rich Christmas
pudding is the perfect way to round off the year.

Roast Beef with Porcini and Roasted Sweet Peppers

A substantial and warming dish for cold, dark evenings.

INGREDIENTS

1.5 kg / 3–3½ lb piece of sirloin
15 ml / 1 tbsp olive oil
450 g / 4 lb small red peppers
115 g / 4 oz mushrooms
175 g / 6 oz thick-sliced pancetta
or smoked bacon, cubed
50 g / 2 oz / 2 tbsp plain flour
150 ml / ¼ pint / ⅔ cup full-
bodied red wine
300 ml / ½ pint / 1¼ cups beef stock
30 ml / 2 tbsp Marsala
10 ml / 2 / tsp dried mixed herbs
salt and freshly ground
black pepper

Serves 8

1

Preheat the oven to 190°C/375°F/
Gas Mark 5. Season the meat well. Heat the
olive oil in a large frying pan. When very
hot, brown the meat on all sides. Place in a
large roasting tin and cook for 1¼ hours.

2

Put the red peppers in the oven to roas
20 minutes, if small ones are available
45 minutes if large ones are used.

3

Near the end of the meat's cooking time,
prepare the gravy. Roughly chop the
mushroom caps and stems.

4

Heat the frying pan again and add the
pancetta or bacon. Cook until the fat runs
freely from the meat. Add the flour and cook
for a few minutes until browned.

5

Gradually stir in the red wine and the st
Bring to the boil, stirring. Lower the h
and add the Marsala, herbs and seasoni

6

Add the mushrooms to the pan and he
through. Remove the sirloin from the c
and leave to stand for 10 minutes befc
carving it. Serve with the roasted pepp
and the hot gravy.

Bacon and Lentil Soup

Serve this hearty soup with chunks of warm, crusty bread.

INGREDIENTS

*450 g / 1 lb thick-sliced
bacon, cubed
1 onion, roughly chopped
1 small turnip, roughly chopped
1 celery stick, chopped
1 carrot, sliced
1 potato, peeled and
roughly chopped
75 g / 3 oz / ½ cup lentils
1 bouquet garni
freshly ground black pepper*

Serves 4

1

Heat a large pan and add the bacon. Cook for
a few minutes, allowing the fat to run out.

2

Add all the vegetables and cook fo
4 minutes.

3

Add the lentils, bouquet garni, seasor
and enough water to cover. Bring to the
and simmer for 1 hour, or until the le
are tender.

Creamy Layered Potatoes

Cook the potatoes on the hob first to help the dish to bake more quickly.

INGREDIENTS

*1.5 kg / 3–3½ lb large potatoes,
peeled and sliced
2 large onions, sliced
75 g / 3 oz 6 tbsp unsalted butter
300 ml / ½ pint / 1¼ cups double
cream
salt and freshly ground
black pepper*

Serves 6

1

Preheat the oven to 200°C/400°F/
Gas Mark 6. Blanch the sliced potatoes for 2
minutes, and drain well. Place the potatoes,
onions, butter and cream in a large pan,
stir well and cook for about 15 minutes.

2

Transfer to an ovenproof dish, season and
bake for 1 hour, until the potatoes are tender.

Traditional Beef Stew and Dumplings

This dish can cook in the oven while you go for a wintery walk to work up an appetite.

INGREDIENTS

25 g / 1 oz / 1 tbsp plain flour
1.2 kg / 2½ lb stewing steak, cubed
30 ml / 2 tbsp olive oil
2 large onions, sliced
450 g / 1 lb carrots, sliced
300 ml / ½ pint / 1¼ cups Guinness or dark beer
3 bay leaves
10 ml / 2 tsp brown sugar
3 fresh thyme sprigs
5 ml / 1 tsp cider vinegar
salt and freshly ground black pepper

For the dumplings
115 g / 4 oz / ½ cup grated hard white fat
225 g / 8 oz / 2 cups self-raising flour
30 ml / 2 tbsp chopped mixed fresh herbs
about 150 ml / ¼ pint / ⅔ cup water

Serves 6

1
Preheat the oven to 160°C/325°F/ Gas Mark 3. Season the flour and sprinkle over the meat, tossing to coat.

2
Heat the oil in a large casserole and ligh sauté the onions and carrots. Remove th vegetables with a slotted spoon and reserve them.

3
Brown the meat well in batches in the casserole.

4
Return all the vegetables to the casserol and add any leftover seasoned flour. Add Guinness or beer, bay leaves, sugar and thyme. Bring the liquid to the boil and t transfer to the oven. Leave the meat to co for 1 hour and 40 minutes, before makin the dumplings.

5
Mix the grated fat, flour and herbs together. Add enough water to make a soft sticky dough.

6
Form the dough into small balls with flou hands. Add the cider vinegar to the meat spoon the dumplings on top. Cook for a further 20 minutes, until the dumpling have cooked through, and serve hot.

Country Pie

A classic raised pie. It takes quite a long time to make,
but is a perfect winter treat.

INGREDIENTS

1 small duck
1 small chicken
350 g / 12 oz pork belly, minced
1 egg, lightly beaten
2 shallots, finely chopped
¹/₂ tsp ground cinnamon
¹/₂ tsp grated nutmeg
5 ml / 1 tsp Worcestershire sauce
finely grated rind of 1 lemon
¹/₂ tsp freshly ground black pepper
150 ml / ¹/₄ pint / ²/₃ cup red wine
175 g / 6 oz ham, cut into cubes
salt and freshly ground
black pepper

For the jelly
all the meat bones and trimmings
2 carrots
1 onion
2 celery sticks
15 ml / 1 tbsp red wine
1 bay leaf
1 whole clove
1 sachet of gelatine
(about 15 g / 1 oz)

For the pastry
225 g / 8 oz / 1 cup hard white fat
300 ml / ¹/₂ pint / 1¹/₄ cups boiling
water
675 g / 1¹/₂ lb / 6 cups plain flour
1 egg, lightly beaten with a
pinch of salt

Serves 12

1

Cut as much meat from the raw duck and chicken as possible, removing the skin and sinews. Cut the duck and chicken breasts into cubes and set them aside.

2

Mix the rest of the duck and chicken me with the minced pork, egg, shallots, spic Worcestershire sauce, lemon rind and sa and pepper. Add the red wine and leave about 15 minutes for the flavours to deve

3

To make the jelly, place the meat bones and trimmings, carrots, onion, celery, wine, bay leaf and clove in a large pan and cover with 2.75 litres / 5 pints / 12¹/₂ cups of water. Bring to the boil, skimming off any scum, and simmer gently for 2¹/₂ hours.

4

To make the pastry, place the fat and wa in a pan and bring to the boil. Sieve the fl and a pinch of salt into a bowl and pour on liquid. Mix with a wooden spoon, and when the dough is cool enough to hand knead it well and let it sit in a warm pla covered with a cloth, for 20–30 minutes until you are ready to use it. Preheat th oven to 200°C / 400°F / Gas Mark 6.

5

se a 25 cm / 10 in loose-based deep cake
Roll out about two-thirds of the pastry
y enough to line the cake tin. Make sure
re are no holes and allow enough pastry
ave a little hanging over the top. Fill the
e with a layer of half the minced-pork
xture; then top this with a layer of the
ed duck and chicken breast-meat and
bes of ham. Top with the remaining
ced pork. Brush the overhanging edges
pastry with water and cover with the
aining rolled-out pastry. Seal the edges
l. Make two large holes in the top and
ecorate with any pastry trimmings.

6

e the pie for 30 minutes. Brush the top
h the egg and salt mixture. Turn down
e oven to 180°C/350°F/Gas Mark 4.
r 30 minutes loosely cover the pie with
to prevent the top getting too brown,
and bake it for a further 1 hour.

7

ain the stock after 2½ hours. Let it cool
remove the solidified layer of fat from
surface. Measure 600 ml/1 pint/2½ cups
ock. Heat it gently to just below boiling
t and whisk the gelatine into it until no
ps are left. Add the remaining strained
stock and leave to cool.

8

en the pie is cool, place a funnel through
of the holes and pour in as much of the
ck as possible, letting it come up to the
les in the crust. Leave to set for at least
24 hours before slicing and serving.

Leek and Onion Tart

This unusual recipe isn't a normal tart with pastry, but an all-in-one savoury slice that is excellent served as an accompaniment to roast meat.

INGREDIENTS

50 g / 2 oz / 4 tbsp unsalted butter
350 g / 12 oz leeks, sliced thinly
225 g / 8 oz 2 cups self-raising flour
115 g / 4 oz / ½ cup grated hard white fat
150 ml / ¼ pint / ⅔ cup water
salt and freshly ground black pepper

Serves 4

1

Preheat the oven to 200°C/400°F/
Gas Mark 6. Melt the butter in a pan
and sauté the leeks until soft. Season well.

2

Mix the flour, fat and water together i
bowl to make a soft but sticky dough
Mix into the leek mixture in the pan. ▶
in a greased shallow ovenproof dish and
for 30 minutes, or until brown and cri
Serve sliced, as a vegetable accompanim

Orange Shortbread Fingers

These are a real tea-time treat. The fingers will keep in an airtight tin for up to two weeks.

115 g / 4 oz / ½ cup unsalted butter, softened
50 g / 2 oz 4 tbsp caster sugar, plus a little extra
finely grated rind of 2 oranges
175 g / 6 oz / 1½ cups plain flour

Makes 18

1

Preheat the oven to 190°C/375°F/ Gas Mark 5. Beat the butter and sugar together until they are soft and creamy. Beat in the orange rind.

2

Gradually add the flour and gently pull the dough together to form a soft ball. Roll the dough out a lightly floured surface until about 1 cm/½ in thick. Cut it into fingers, sprinkle over a little extra caster sugar, prick with a fork and bake for about 20 minutes, or until the fingers are a light golden colour.

Cranberry Muffins

A tea or breakfast dish that is not too sweet.

INGREDIENTS

350 g / 12 oz / 3 cups plain flour
15 ml / 1 tsp baking powder
pinch of salt
115 g / 4 oz / ½ cup caster sugar
2 eggs
150 ml 1¼ pint / ⅔ cup milk
50 ml / 2 fl oz / 4 tbsp corn oil
finely grated rind of 1 orange
150 g / 5 oz cranberries

Makes 12

1

Preheat the oven to 190°C/375°F/
Gas Mark 5. Line 12 deep muffin tins with
paper cases. Mix the flour, baking powder,
salt and caster sugar together.

2

Lightly beat the eggs with the milk and
Add them to the dry ingredients and b
to make a smooth batter. Stir in the ora
rind and cranberries. Divide the mixt
between the muffin cases and bake fo
25 minutes until risen and golden.
Leave to cool in the tins for a few minu
and serve warm or cold.

Scotch Pancakes

Serve these while still warm, with butter and jam.

INGREDIENTS

225 g / 8 oz / 2 cups self-raising
flour
50 g / 2 oz / 4 tbsp caster sugar
50 g / 2 oz / 4 tbsp butter, melted
1 egg
300 ml / ½ pint / 1¼ cups milk
15 g / ½ oz / 1 tbsp hard white fat

Makes 24

1

Mix the flour and sugar together. Add the
melted butter and egg with two-thirds of the
milk. Mix to a smooth batter – it should be
thin enough to find its own level.

2

Heat a griddle or a heavy-based frying
and wipe it with a little hard white fa
When hot, drop spoonfuls of the mixtu
on to the hot griddle or pan. When bub
come to the surface of the pancakes, flip t
over to cook until golden on the other s
Keep the pancakes warm wrapped in a
towel while cooking the rest of the mixt

Christmas Pudding

The classic Christmas dessert. Wrap it in muslin and store it in an airtight container for up to a year for the flavours to develop.

INGREDIENTS

115 g / 4 oz / 1 cup plain flour
pinch of salt
5 ml / 1 tsp ground mixed spice
½ tsp ground cinnamon
¼ tsp freshly grated nutmeg
225 g / 8 oz / 1 cup grated hard white fat
1 dessert apple, grated
225 g / 8 oz / 2 cups fresh white breadcrumbs
350 g / 12 oz / 1⅛ cups soft brown sugar
50 g / 2 oz flaked almonds
225 g / 8 oz / 1½ cups seedless raisins
225 g / 8 oz / 1½ cups currants
225 g / 8 oz / 1½ cups sultanas
115 g / 4 oz ready-to-eat dried apricots
115 g / 4 oz / ¾ cup chopped mixed peel
finely grated rind and juice of 1 lemon
30 ml / 2 tbsp black treacle
3 eggs
300 ml / ½ pint / 1¼ cups milk
30 ml / 2 tbsp rum

Serves 8

1

Sieve the flour, salt and spices into a large bowl.

2

Add the fat, apple and other dry ingredie including the grated lemon rind.

3

Heat the treacle until warm and runny and pour into the dry ingredients.

4

Mix together the eggs, milk, rum and lemon juice.

5

Stir the liquid into the dry mixture.

6

Spoon the mixture into two 1.2 litre 2 pint / 5 cup basins. Overwrap the puddings with pieces of greaseproof pap pleated to allow for expansion, and tie w string. Steam the puddings in a steamer saucepan of boiling water. Each puddin needs 10 hours' cooking and 3 hours reheating. Remember to keep the water topped up to keep the pans from boiling Serve decorated with holly.

Gifts from the Pantry

Make the most of seasonal fruits and vegetables,
by making jams, jellies and preserves to enjoy
the year round, or to give as gifts.
Country favourites include strawberry jam,
apple or mint jelly, or piccalilli.

Apple and Mint Jelly

This jelly is delicious served with garden peas, as well as the more traditional rich roasted meat such as lamb.

INGREDIENTS

900 g / 2 lb Bramley cooking apples
granulated sugar
45 ml / 3 tbsp chopped fresh mint

Makes 3 × 450g / 1 lb jars

1

Chop the apples roughly and put them in a preserving pan.

2

Add enough water to cover. Simmer unt the fruit is soft.

3

Pour through a jelly bag, allowing it to drip overnight. Do not squeeze the bag or the jelly will become cloudy.

4

Measure the amount of juice. To every 600ml / 1 pint/2½ cups of juice, add 500g/1¼ lb/2¾ cups granulated sugar.

5

Place the juice and sugar in a large pan an heat gently. Dissolve the sugar and then bring to the boil. Test for setting, by pouring about 15 ml/1 tbsp into a sauc and leaving to cool slightly. If a wrinkle forms on the surface when pushed with fingertip, the jelly will set. When a set i reached, leave to cool.

6

Stir in the mint and pot into sterilized jar Seal each jar with a waxed disc and a tigh fitting cellophane top. Store in a cool, dark place. The jelly will keep unopene for up to a year. Once opened, keep in th fridge and consume within a week.

Lemon and Lime Curd

Serve this creamy, tangy spread with toast or muffins,
instead of jam, for a delightful change.

INGREDIENTS

115 g/4 oz/½ cup
unsalted butter
3 eggs

grated rind and juice of 2 lemons
grated rind and juice of 2 limes
225 g/8 oz/1⅛ cups caster sugar

Makes 2 × 450g/1 lb jars

1

Set a heatproof mixing bowl over a large pan
of simmering water. Add the butter.

2

Lightly beat the eggs and add them
to the butter.

3

Add the lemon and lime rinds and juices
then add the sugar.

4

Stir the mixture constantly until it thickens.
Pour into sterilized jars. Seal each jar with a
waxed disc and a tightly fitting cellophane top.
Store in a cool, dark place. The curd will
keep unopened for up to a month.
Once opened, keep in the fridge and
consume within a week.

Poached Spiced Plums in Brandy

Bottling spiced fruit is a great way to preserve summer flavours for eating in winter. Serve these with whipped cream as a dessert.

INGREDIENTS

600 ml / 1 pint / 2½ cups brandy
rind of 1 lemon, peeled in a
long strip
350 g / 12 oz / 1⅔ cups
caster sugar
1 cinnamon stick
900 g / 2 lb fresh plums

Makes 900 g / 2 lb

1

Put the brandy, lemon rind, sugar and cinnamon stick in a large pan and heat gently to dissolve the sugar. Add the plums and poach for 15 minutes, or until soft. Remove with a slotted spoon.

2

Reduce the syrup by a third by rapid boi
Strain it over the plums. Bottle the plu
in large sterilized jars. Seal tightly and s
for up to 6 months in a cool, dark plac

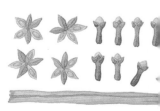

Spiced Pickled Pears

These delicious pears are the perfect accompaniment for cooked ham or cold meat salads.

INGREDIENTS

900 g / 2 lb pears
600 ml / 1 pint / 2½ cups
white-wine vinegar
225 g / 8 oz / 1⅛ cups caster sugar
1 cinnamon stick
5 star anise
10 whole cloves

Makes 900 g / 2 lb

1

Peel the pears, keeping them whole and leaving on the stalks. Heat the vinegar and sugar together until the sugar has melted. Pour over the pears and poach for 15 minutes.

2

Add the cinnamon, star anise and cloves and simmer for 10 minutes. Remove the pears and pack tightly into sterilized jars. Simmer the syrup for a further 15 minutes and pour it over the pears. Seal the jars tightly and store in a cool, dark place. The pears will keep for up to a year unopened. Once opened, store in the fridge and consume within a week.

Tomato Chutney

*This spicy chutney is delicious with a selection of cheeses and biscuits,
or with cold meats.*

INGREDIENTS

900 g/2 lb tomatoes, skinned
225 g/8 oz/1⅓ cups raisins
225 g/8 oz onions, chopped

225 g/8 oz/1⅛ cups caster sugar
600 ml/1 pint/2½ cups
malt vinegar

Makes 4 × 450 g/1 lb jars

1

Chop the tomatoes roughly. Put them in
a preserving pan.

2

Add the raisins, onions and caster sugar.

3

Pour over the vinegar. Bring to the b
and let it simmer for 2 hours, uncover
Pot into sterilized jars. Seal with a waxed
and cover with a tightly fitting celloph
top. Store in a cool, dark place. The chu
will keep unopened for up to a year. O
opened, store in the fridge and consur
within a week.

Strawberry Jam

This classic recipe is always popular. Make sure the jam is allowed to cool before pouring into jars so the fruit doesn't float to the top.

INGREDIENTS

1.5 kg/3–3½ lb strawberries
juice of ½ lemon
1.5 kg/3–3½ lb granulated sugar

Makes about 2.25 kg/5 lb

1

Hull the strawberries.

2

Put the strawberries in a pan with the lemon juice. Mash a few of the strawberr Let the fruit simmer for 20 minutes o until softened.

3

Add the sugar and let it dissolve slowly over a gentle heat. Then let the jam boil rapidly until a setting point is reached.

4

Leave to stand until the strawberries a well distributed through the jam. Pot ir sterilized jars. Seal each jar with a waxed and cover with a tightly fitting cellopha top. Store in a cool dark place. The jar may be kept unopened for up to a year Once opened, keep in the fridge and consume within a week.

Three-fruit Marmalade

*Home-made marmalade may be time-consuming but the results are
incomparably better than store-bought varieties.*

INGREDIENTS

350 g/12 oz oranges
350 g/12 oz lemons
700 g/1½ lb grapefruit
*2.5 litres/4½ pints/10¼ cups
water*
2.75 kg/6 lb granulated sugar

Makes 6 × 450/1 lb jars

1

Rinse and dry the fruit.

2

Put the fruit in a preserving pan. Add t
water and let it simmer for about 2 hou

3

Quarter the fruit, remove the pulp and
add it to the pan with the cooking liquid.

4

Cut the rinds into slivers, and add to the p
Add the sugar. Gently heat until the sug
has dissolved. Bring to the boil and cool
until a setting point is reached. Leave to
stand for 1 hour to allow the peel to sett
Pour into sterilized jars. Seal each jar wit
a waxed disc and a tightly fitting cellopha
top. Store in a cool, dark place.

Piccalilli

The piquancy of this relish partners well with sausages, bacon or ham.

INGREDIENTS

675 g / 1½ lb cauliflower
450 g / 1 lb small onions
350 g / 12 oz French beans
5 ml / 1 tsp ground turmeric

5 ml / 1 tsp dry mustard powder
10 ml / 2 tsp cornflour
600 ml / 1 pint / 2½ cups vinegar

Makes 3 × 450 g / 1 lb jars

1

Cut the cauliflower into tiny florets.

2

Peel the onions and top and tail
the French beans.

3

In a small saucepan, measure in the turm
mustard powder and cornflour, and po
over the vinegar. Stir well and simme
for 10 minutes.

4

Pour the vinegar mixture over the vegetables
in a pan, mix well and simmer
for 45 minutes.

5

Pour into sterilized jars. Seal each jar wi
waxed disc and a tightly fitting celloph
top. Store in a cool dark place. The picc
will keep unopened for up to a year. O
opened store in the fridge and consur
within a week.

Rosemary-flavoured Oil

This pungent oil is ideal drizzled over meat or vegetables before grilling.

INGREDIENTS

600 ml / 1 pint / 2½ cups olive oil
5 fresh rosemary sprigs

Makes 600 ml / 1 pint / 2½ cups

1

Heat the oil until warm but not too hot.

2

Add four rosemary sprigs and heat gen[...]
Put the reserved rosemary sprig in a cl[...]
bottle. Strain the oil, pour in the bottle[...]
seal tightly. Allow to cool and store in[...]
cool, dark place. Use within a week.

Thyme-flavoured Vinegar

This vinegar is delicious sprinkled over salmon intended for poaching.

INGREDIENTS

600 ml / 1 pint / 2½ cups
white-wine vinegar
5 fresh thyme sprigs
3 garlic cloves, peeled

Makes 600 ml / 1 pint / 2½ cups

1

Warm the vinegar.

2

Add four thyme sprigs and the garlic a[...]
heat gently. Put the reserved thyme spri[...]
a clean bottle, strain the vinegar, and ad[...]
the bottle. Seal tightly, allow to cool a[...]
store in a cool, dark place. The vinega[...]
may be kept unopened for up to 3 mont[...]

Index

INDEX

Acknowledgements

Tessa Evelegh would like to thank Lindsay Porter for all her
inspiration and encouragement in putting this book together;
Practical Gardening magazine for all their support; Michelle
Garrett for her wonderful, vibrant photographs; and James and
Madeleine for their encouragement and friendship.

Tessa and the publishers would also like to thank Fiona
Barnett at Manic Botanic for the wheat heart on page 120
Eileen Simpson at Hill Farm Herbs for supplying the
dried-herb wreath on page 136; and Somerset House of Iro▮
for the chair featured on page 19.

Suppliers

Bear Woods Supply Co. Inc.
P.O. Box 275
Cornwallis
Nova Scotia B0S 1H0
Canada
(tel: 800-565-5066; fax: 888-599-1118;
web: www.bearwood.com)
Suppliers of a wide range of wooden dowels
and rods, fluted dowel pins, Shaker pegs,
furniture spindles and finials, wood hearts
and star cut-outs, wood candle cups and
much more

Hill Farm Herbs
Park Walk
Brigstock
Kettering
Northamptonshire
NN14 3HH, UK
(tel: 01536 373694)
Suppliers of potted fresh herbs, dried herbs
and flowers, and dried flower decorations

Farrow & Ball
Uddens Estate
Wimborne
Dorset BH21 7NL, UK
(web: www.farrow-ball.com)
Suppliers of National Trust paints

TheFlowerMart.com
P.O. Box 1809
Hillsboro OR 97123
USA
(tel: 1-503-628-3167 or 1-800-733-0506;
fax: 1-503-628-0647)
Dried flower specialists

The Folk Art Factory
PO Box 298
Bull Creek
Western Australia 6149
(tel: +61 8 9310 5923;
fax: +61 8 9310 5924)
Folk and decorative art supplies

Manic Botanic
Fairfax House
15 Fulwood Place
Holborn
London WC1V 6AY, UK
(tel: 020 7978 4505)
Suppliers of made-to-order floral deco▮

Robert Young Antiques
68 Battersea Bridge Road
London SW11 3AG, UK
(tel: 020 7228 7847; fax: 020 7585 0▮
web: www.robertyoungantiques.com)

Shaker Ltd
72–73 Marylebone High Street
London W1U 5JW, UK
(tel: 020 7935 9461)
Hand-made Shaker furniture from
sustainable sources, gifts and home
accessories ranging from Shaker boxes,
quilts and blankets to folk-art birds

NOTES

NOTES

NOTES

NOTES

NOTES

NOTES

NOTES

NOTES